THE LIVING MILTON

THE LIVING MILTON

Essays by Various Hands
Collected and Edited by

FRANK KERMODE

ROUTLEDGE & KEGAN PAUL
London

First published 1960
by Routledge & Kegan Paul Ltd
Broadway House, 68-74 Carter Lane, E.C.4

Printed in Great Britain
by Lowe & Brydone (Printers) Ltd
London, N.W.10

Second impression 1962
Third impression 1963
Fourth impression 1967

© *Routledge & Kegan Paul Ltd 1960*

No part of this book may be reproduced in any form without permission from the publisher, except for the quotation of brief passages in criticism

B60-15401

vagliami il lungo studio e il grande amore
che m'ha fatto cercar lo tuo volume.

CONTENTS

PREFACE

THE contributors to this collection, known admirers of Milton, were not invited to produce eulogies, much as I should have liked to issue the command: '*Onorate l'altissimo Poeta*'. They have some other characteristics in common. All save one are university teachers (five at the ancient, four at the modern universities) and the exception is John Wain, who was in the business until a few years ago. Almost all of them are best known for their work in the criticism of later literature than Milton, one might almost say the literature of our own time. Half of them are well known as poets. Their average age is well under forty. They may be taken, without affectation, as representing something new in the history of Milton criticism in this country; they exhibit an increasing, though not absolute, independence of the great controversy which dominated Milton studies until recently. It is not that they have disposed of the charges brought against the poet by a generation of Miltonoclasts; perhaps, as Bernard Bergonzi suggests, this cannot be done. But however guarded their admiration, they have no evident disposition to acquiesce in that 'dislodgement' of the poet which was supposed to have been effected a generation back 'with surprisingly little fuss'. On the other hand, they show small interest in the methods of defence employed during the same period by Miltonolaters; and J. B. Broadbent, in the most technical of these essays, is clear that he must dispense with the brilliant assistance of Miss Rosemund Tuve, a leading exponent of defence by scholarship. I think it fair to say that all the contributors have found it possible to include Milton in a characteristically modern view of literature, to treat him as a living poet.

This is the sole explanation of certain coincidences of tone and opinion in these essays. They are not due to collusion or to editorial interference. They will not obscure the fact that there is also much disagreement. I myself was surprised to discover that some points I made in my own tendentious contribution were made also by David Daiches and Bernard Bergonzi; but with much that they say I sharply disagree, and I find myself arguing against other contributors also, notably Donald Davie and W. W. Robson. It is hoped that such disagreements will be fruitful. Milton needs to be discussed in new ways.

Unless otherwise stated, the Everyman edition of B. A. Wright (Dent, 1956) is used throughout in quotations from the poems.

FRANK KERMODE

I

STRENGTH AND ISOLATION: PESSIMISTIC NOTES OF A MILTONOLATER

John Wain

MILTON'S IS a poetry of the will. Its most characteristic theme is the clash of wills; his long narrative and dramatic poems all deal with disputes; he is always showing us how one person tried to win another to his point of view, and how it was that he succeeded or failed. In procedure, too, this is poetry in which will-power is very evident. It might be described—baldly, but not, I think, inaccurately, and certainly with no satiric intention—as a battle of wills between Milton and the English language.

Shakespeare had given English its head. He had ranged over every kind of English spoken in his day, from the most demotic to the most statesmanlike, from comic malapropisms to the aureate conversation of scholars, and made of them a dramatic poetry which allowed for every possibility, expressed every nuance, dealt with every situation. That Milton was aware of Shakespeare's greatness is sufficiently attested by the fact that he wrote a poem describing his relics as 'hallowed'. Nevertheless, it is equally evident that Milton had an attitude towards Shakespeare that can best be described as defensive. He made a slightly self-important fuss about deciding to write in English ('Hail native language, that by sinews weak' etc.), as if still conscious of a lingering doubt as to whether English had the dignity and permanence to measure up to great work. To hesitate in this way about a language that has already had its greatest classic, as if *Hamlet* and *King Lear* were still not quite conclusive evidence that English was ready for great works of the imagination, is, we may fairly say, defensive. And the whole direction that Milton's genius took—bookish, prescriptive, unremittingly didactic—reflects very exactly the position of a poet determined to enrich English with major work, conscious of his ability to do so, and yet aware that a huge piece of the available territory had already been staked. His best plan would be to build something really permanent on the part that remained, and this Milton has done.

There had been learned, as distinct from popular, poets in English before; Milton would know well enough that both Chaucer and Spenser had been concerned to make English do what the languages of more civilized nations had already done. But both were obsolete; the taste of the learned world had since hardened and systematized itself, not thereafter to budge for two and a half centuries. Milton belonged to the first generation of fully-qualified, card-carrying classical scholars, as Housman did to the last; he had the literary tastes and interests of that powerful enclave who dominated Western European education unbrokenly from his day to ours. Given a little time to catch up with the latest work, he could have walked straight into a classical professorship in Jowett's day. (There is an emendation of Milton's in the received text of the *Bacchae* of Euripides.) He was the first, and immeasurably the greatest of the 'scholar-poets', as that term was delimited and defined by the eighteenth and nineteenth centuries.

But of course that was only one of the things he was. The great humanist was also the great Puritan, the supreme poetic voice of English Puritanism. The two ideals are not necessarily in discord; at any rate, whatever discords there may have been at the time, they appear from this distance to have resolved themselves satisfactorily enough. Puritanism is a religion of the will, of the individual conscience, almost (one might say) of self-reliance. If the Puritan cannot make his peace with God out of the scrupulousness of his own soul, there is no one who can do it for him. And if the learned humanist poet, seeking to make English repeat the lessons it has learnt from Latin and Greek, cannot find the necessary authority within his own scholarship and taste, there is no one who can help him.

I do not see why we should be afraid to attempt a short description of Milton's poetic style. Its essence seems to me to reside in two things: music and emphasis. The music, we may take for granted. Not even Shakespeare had more. The emphasis is part of his habit of mind; he *will* lead the reader, and the language, in the direction he wants them to go at the moment; no resistance is possible. When Satan first lands on Earth to begin the corruption of Adam and Eve,

> horror and doubt distract
> His troubl'd thoughts, and from the bottom stirr
> The Hell within him, for within him Hell
> He brings, and round about him, nor from Hell
> One step no more than from himself can fly
> By change of place: Now conscience wakes despair
> That slumberd, wakes the bitter memorie
> Of what he was, what is, and what must be
> Worse; of worse deeds worse sufferings must ensue!
>
> (iv. 18–26)

The repetitions here (*Hell* three times in two lines, *wakes* twice in two lines, *what* and *worse* both three times in a line), are no mere echo of a Latin stylistic trick; they hammer home the ominous nature of what is happening.

What else? 'His natural port is a gigantic loftiness,' of course. Milton does not fly, he soars. But in allowing the truth of this, the first and most obvious judgment to occur to anyone coming to Milton for the first time, we must add also that he was one of our greatest masters of the plain style. He knew how to write that utterly bare, poignant poetry which is reached by paring away everything except the final words that make the final sense.

> So saying, her rash hand in evil hour
> Forth reaching to the Fruit, she pluckd, she eat:
> Earth felt the wound, and Nature from her seate
> Sighing through all her Works gave signs of woe,
> That all was lost.
>
> (ix. 780–84)

> Lift not thy spear against the Muses Bowr,
> The great *Emathian* Conqueror bid spare
> The house of *Pindarus*, when Temple and Towr

Went to the ground: And the repeated air
Of sad *Electra*'s Poet had the power
To save th' *Athenian* Walls from ruin bare.
(Sonnet viii)

All otherwise to me my thoughts portend,
That these dark orbs no more shall treat with light,
Nor th' other light of life continue long,
But yield to double darkness nigh at hand;
So much I feel my genial spirits droop,
My hopes all flat, nature within me seems
In all her functions weary of herself;
My race of glory run, and race of shame,
And I shall shortly be with them that rest.
(*Samson Agonistus*, 590–98)

These passages could hardly be in plainer, less pompous English; what makes them 'Miltonic' is the spare, severe elegance that dictates the choice both of words and rhythms.

The parallel is, clearly, with Yeats, another poet whose manner is often described as lofty and grand, and sometimes, by hostile critics, called inflated, but who turns out on inspection to be not in the least afraid of plain, familiar language.

Two thoughts were so mixed up I could not tell
Whether of her or God he thought the most,
But think that his mind's eye,
When upward turned, on one sole image fell;
And that a slight companionable ghost,
Wild with divinity,
Had so lit up the whole
Immense miraculous house
The Bible promised us,
It seemed a gold-fish swimming in a bowl.

The real virtuosity of Yeats is that he can get away with an expression like 'mixed up', which is utterly casual, in a poem whose tone is rapt, lofty, hieratic. After this, it comes as no surprise that he can invoke harmlessly a domestic image, the gold-fish swimming round in its bowl, to convey Horton's ecstatic vision of the blessed state of the woman he loved.

Naturally, the resemblance between these two great poets is not only stylistic. (It never is.) They write in a similar way because they have a temperamental affinity. Both were shy, proud men who forced themselves, not without a self-consuming inner delight, to play a part on the public stage. Both were in love with pride—Milton half-consciously, Yeats openly—and both wrote superbly in praise of the proud character. Yeats even uses the word 'arrogant' as a term of praise.

> Maud Gonne at Howth station waiting for a train,
> Pallas Athene in that straight back and arrogant head.

Since arrogance is in fact an unpleasant characteristic, one is driven to ask how Yeats manages to enlist our sympathy, even momentarily, for people who suffer from it. And the answer comes quickly. These people are on the losing side. The impoverished Irish gentry, who helped Yeats to do his life's work, were going down before the advance of modern bureaucracy and commerce; the politician and the 'huckster', both egalitarian and rationalistic though in conflicting ways, were inexorably treading the 'renowned generations' into the mire. This, of course, is the major theme of Yeats's poems, and it is what reconciles one to the endlessly asserted *hauteur* of the characters he writes about. Pride such as theirs would be intolerable in a governing class that was actually dominant.

Milton is in exactly the same position. Eleven years ago, discussing Dr. Rajan's book on Milton,[1] I wrote *à propos* the character of Satan, 'Defeat is the only thing that can make pride beautiful'; and after all these years I cannot think of a better formulation. Satan, when we first see him, is unforgettably beautiful and heroic, because he has lost everything and is still proud. It is only later in the poem, when we get to know him better and realize that this pride is inseparable from his character, that he was proud even in blessedness and would be so even in victory, that we turn against him. It has been suggested that Satan's character deteriorates as the poem goes on; it would be nearer the mark to say that the character stays the same, but Milton turns it round to show it in an increasingly harsh light. All in all, the portrait of Satan is so flawless and yet so powerful that it strikes one as almost miraculous. Only a proud man could have

[1] *Mandrake,* No. 6 (1947).

written it, a man who knew what it was to be persecuted and to confront his persecutors with pride, and to see the ruin of his hopes and still be proud.

> Bred to a harder thing
> Than triumph, turn away,
> And like a laughing string
> Whereon mad fingers play
> Amid a place of stone,
> Be secret and exult
> Because of all things known
> That is most difficult.

The same temperament that enabled Milton to succeed so unforgettably in his portrait of Satan worked against him, of course, when it came to portraying God the Father. About his efforts in this direction, the less said the better. Probably it is impossible to portray the Deity in imaginative literature, except as a vaguely but powerfully apprehended presence. And Milton was writing a classical epic, within which there was no room for anything so misty. It had to be tackled frontally, and the result was a failure. But even had the task been possible, we could hardly expect Milton to succeed in it. He lacked the power to imagine a God at once omnipotent and genuinely lovable. In fact, to me, the chief interest of Milton's portrait of God the Father (as of his portrait of God the Son in *Paradise Regained*) is autobiographical. When God enjoys a good laugh at the futile ingenuity of the fallen angels, we see a glimpse of the Milton who, in private life, loved nothing so much as a joke at the expense of a slow-witted person ('Extreme pleasant in his conversation, & at dinner, supper &c; but Satyrical'). Indeed, a high proportion of our meagre information about Milton's personal life concerns this propensity for witty mockery. There is Richardson's anecdote about how he would make fun of that stupid, honest servant of his, who went to Presbyterian meetings and came home with a garbled account of what had been said; and there is the Greek inscription he caused to be engraved round his portrait. (The joke was that the artist, not understanding Greek, himself painstakingly engraved round the edge of the portrait an unflattering judgment of its merit.) Milton's idea of a joke, in other words, was to see somebody make a fool of himself. In everything else he transcended the merely donnish character; in this one respect he was a High Table natural.

'His verse as one reads it seems something necessary and eternal.' Those words of Hopkins can stand as a token of the volume upon volume of praise lavished on Milton by his fellow English poets. (Very few of *them*, certainly, found *Paradise Lost* 'as mechanical as bricklaying'. But then bricklaying is not mechanical.) Milton has always appealed to poets, and it is impossible to imagine an English poet who did not find his work, at the very least, instructive and stimulating. But with the ordinary reader, the twentieth century is very much Milton's period 'out'. So far out, indeed, that one doubts whether anything short of a titanic revolution in taste will bring him back in. The reason for this neglect is an honourable one to Milton, and for that matter it reflects no particular discredit on the modern reader. It is simply that one of his chief virtues has come to be regarded as a vice. Milton has an extraordinary power of sustaining large structures. He can strike the right tone for what he wants to say and then keep within that tone for page after page, book after book. But this is exactly what the modern reader does not want him to do. The modern ear is attuned entirely to short, concentrated poems. If a poet attempts a long poem, he will find himself addressing the empty air unless he adopts a deliberately discontinuous method. A few snatches of this, a pinch of that; the page must be broken up as relentlessly as the page of a newspaper.

There is probably nothing to be done about this. It is simply a fact. The modern sensibility works in naturally with a medium like the cinema, with its endless fading-in and fading-out, its tracking, panning and all the rest of the devices for keeping dimension and angle in a continually shifting state. The moving picture hit England during the First World War, and by 1922 English literature already had a masterpiece of cinematic poetry, *The Waste Land*. Pound, in the Cantos, has gone on from that day to this building a long poem on the principle of the film. That is the way the stream is flowing, has been flowing for thirty-five years, and we can never hope to reverse it merely by preaching. Symbolism on the one hand, the cinema on the other; concentration and discontinuity. Even the theatre has had to adopt cinematic techniques in order to survive—though this is not the same problem in England as in France, since Shakespeare, the founding father of English drama, himself used cinematic techniques, though for different reasons. But can one imagine a Racinian play —not a revival, but a new play that proceeded on genuine Racinian lines—succeeding on the stage today? What would become of those tirades that build upward and upward and *never* seem to flag?

Milton is with Racine, rather than with Shakespeare. One of his great powers is the power of sustaining a homogeneous style. Everyone who writes knows how difficult this is; but the modern reader's reaction is the Johnsonian 'Sir, I wish it had been impossible.'

There is only one way out, and I think I know what it is. The other day I happened to look, for the first time in twenty years, at that preposterous work *The Oxford Dictionary of Quotations,* the method of whose amiable compiler, as you recall, was to go through English literature and snip out all the well-known phrases, arranging them according to author rather than subject. Under 'Milton' then, we find several pages of discrete lines and phrases. This kind of thing:

> Our torments also may in length of time
> Become our elements.

> With grave
> Aspect he rose, and in his rising seem'd
> A pillar of state; deep on his front engraven
> Deliberation sat and public care;
> And princely counsel in his face yet shone,
> Majestic though in ruin.

> To sit in darkness here,
> Hatching vain empires.

> Who shall tempt with wand'ring feet
> The dark unbottomed infinite abyss
> And through the palpable obscure find out
> His uncouth way.

> Long is the way
> And hard, that out of hell leads up to light.

O shame to men! Devil with devil damn'd
Firm concord holds, men only disagree
Of creatures rational.

In discourse more sweet
(For eloquence the soul, song charms the sense,)
Others apart sat on a hill retir'd,
In thoughts more elevate, and reason'd high
Of providence, foreknowledge, will, and fate,
Fix'd fate, free will, foreknowledge absolute,
And found no end, in wand'ring mazes lost.

Vain wisdom all, and false philosophy.

A gulf profound as that Serbonian bog
Betwixt Damiata and Mount Casius old,
Where armies whole have sunk: the parching air
Burns frore, and cold performs th' effect of fire.

The bitter change
Of fierce extremes, extremes by change more fierce.

O'er many a frozen, many a fiery Alp,
Rocks, caves, lakes, ferns, bogs, dens, and shades of
death.

In all seriousness, if I wanted to convert a modern reader of poetry to the view that Milton was a great poet, I would start by showing him these pages in the Dictionary. If one could get into his head that Milton's long poems, far from being merely unreadable, were a quarry in which one could pick up such jewels as these, he might turn to them. And once having turned, he might —just might—find, as he read on, that Milton's sustaining power, his unflagging homogeneity, was not merely an irritating mannerism but a strength. Perhaps we should try the experiment. If those pages from the Dictionary were reprinted, just as they stand, under the title of 'Milton's Cantos', they might enjoy a vogue which would lead a few hardy spirits to attempt the poems in their entirety. Perhaps some publisher will oblige. Until then, we must simply admit the regrettable fact that our second greatest poet will never have a wide modern audience, simply because the form in which he worked has died and nothing seems to revive it.

There is a further problem, which goes too far outside our present framework to be more than indicated. If the long poem has died, the long religious poem has not only died but vanished beyond even the possibility of a tomb. Great poetry can still be written about religious belief and the religious emotions; one has no fear that this will die out; but the treatment of religious, or at any rate Christian, belief in narrative verse was a by-product of the assumption that the Bible, being by a divine Author, was the most exalted book the human mind could conceive, and that if a mere mortal wished to handle the same subject he must do so in epic verse. Nowadays the literary mind seems unable to use mythology, sacred or otherwise, except in burlesque form. Nothing will bridge the gap between the presentation of God the Father in *Paradise Lost* and in, say, Marc Connolly's *Green Pastures*. It is not a literary but a social, almost an anthropological, difference.

None of this need appal the reader who has any historical sense; and perhaps even at the simpler levels of appreciation Milton may still find a welcome among older people. For a society not very different from the seventeenth-century Puritans, lived on in several European countries and doubtless in America, until almost within living memory. The young Gide, it will be recalled, once knocked at a cottage door when benighted in the countryside near Uzès, and found a Huguenot family with exactly that stern simplicity of manners:

> In the meantime the children came in from work—a grown-up girl and three boys; more delicately built than their grandfather; good-looking young people, but with grave faces for their age, and even perhaps a touch of sternness on their brows. Their mother placed the steaming soup on the table and stopped me in the middle of a sentence with a quiet motion of her hand, while the old man said the *benedicite*.
>
> It was during supper that he spoke of my grandfather; his language, though precise, was full of imagery; I am sorry not to have noted down some of his phrases. 'Can this be really nothing but a family of peasants?' I kept saying to myself. 'What distinction they have, what vivacity, what dignity compared to our loutish, stolid Normandy labourers!' At the end

of supper, I got up to go; but my hosts would not hear of it. The mother was already setting about her preparations; the eldest son would sleep with one of his brothers; I should have his room and his bed, which she spread with clean coarse sheets smelling deliciously of lavender. With them, she said, it was early to bed and early to rise, but as for me, I might sit up and read, if I felt inclined to.

'But,' said the old man, 'you will allow us to follow our usual custom—which will not astonish you, as you are Monsieur Tancrède's grandson.'

Then he fetched down the big Bible I had noticed, and put it on the table which had been cleared. His daughter and grandchildren sat down again on either side of him at the table in an attitude of devotion that came naturally to them. The grandfather opened the Holy Book and read aloud a chapter of the Gospels in a solemn voice, and then a psalm; after which, they all, with the exception of himself, knelt down in front of their chairs. I saw that he remained standing, with his eyes shut and his hands laid on the closed book. He uttered a short prayer of thanksgiving, very dignified and very simple, with no requests in it, and I remember he thanked God for leading me to his door, and in such a tone that my whole heart responded to his words. To end up with, he said the Lord's Prayer; then there was a moment's silence before each of the children rose. It was all so noble and so calm, the kiss of peace he put on the forehead of each so beautiful, that I too went up with the others and in my turn offered him my forehead.[1]

The household in which Milton was reared must have been like a more refined, bookish version of that which so impressed Gide; and all of us can remember old people who seemed to preserve something of that old Protestant simplicity and dignity. Has the type vanished utterly? If so, that makes the study of Milton not a mere scholarly pastime, but an urgent task, before an immense and essential portion of the European past becomes unintelligible for ever.

[1] *Si le grain ne meurt,* cap. 2 (Dorothy Bussy's translation).

II

THE NATIVITY ODE

J. B. Broadbent

JOHNSON IGNORED the Ode and most subsequent critics have merely regretted the conceit about the sun in bed. But, since Cook's annotations,[1] specialist scholars have treated it with increasing respect; so that now, just as *Paradise Lost* is seen as consummating thirteen centuries of hexameral writing, the Ode is set at the end of a tradition of late-classical and neo-Latin celebrations of the nativity. Elements of the tradition are traced in works by Spenser, Giles Fletcher, Beaumont, and Donne; but poems outside that tradition—medieval carols, and vernacular Renaissance poems on the nativity by Southwell, Jonson, Herbert, Crashaw, Drummond, Vaughan, Herrick—are regarded as minor insularities.[2] It is this being absolute for tradition that I

[1] 'Notes on Milton's N.O.", *Trans. Connecticut Acad. Arts & Sciences,* XV (1909), 307–68. I get no help from later studies except D. C. Allen's in his *Harmonious Vision* (Baltimore, 1954), and Miss Tuve's cited below.

[2] Spenser: 'Hymne of Heauenly Loue', 134 ff. G. Fletcher: *Christ's Victory in Heaven,* lxxviii ff. (highly rhetorical and suitably decorated with sentimental designs). Beaumont: *Psyche*, vii. Donne: 'Annunciation' and 'Nativitie' in *La Corona*. Southwell: 'The Burning Babe'. Jonson: 'Hymn on the Nativity of my Saviour'. Herbert: 'Christmas'. Crashaw: Nativity and Epiphany hymns and parts of the hymn to Jesus, epigrams (e.g. 'On the B. Virgins bashfulnesse') and parts of his trans. of the *Sospetto d'Herode*; Crashaw also has some Latin epigrams on nativity motifs, and the rhetorical-conceited elegiacs *Deus sub utero virginis* and *In nocturnum & hyemale iter infantis Domini.* Drummond: 'Run, shepherds, run' in *Flowers of Zion* and short hymns to the Virgin and on the nativity in *Divine Poems* (much duller than Crashaw).

challenge here. I shall try to avoid complaining that the Ode is not 'Away in a manger': Milton's poetry, as Arnold, acknowledged, is emetic of deliquescent romanticism. But as Arnold also noted,[1] distinctions of value and kind may be smudged by historical as much as personal interest. As ideography grows more correct we are tempted to acknowledge traditions of symbolism and ideology without criticizing their quality, or the quality of the poetry they authorize; and in a period of religious neo-orthodoxy we may (so many traditions being religious) even allow a personal interest in the tradition to impute extra authority to it and to its uses in poetry.

I write mainly in response to the stimulus of Miss Rosemond Tuve's essay on '*The Hymn* on the Morning of Christ's Nativity' in her *Images and Themes in Five Poems by Milton* (1957). Miss Tuve's learning, and her sensitivity to Milton's verse, are enviable; but it seems to me that her delight in the traditional materials makes her over-value Milton's management of them, and prevents her evaluating the choice he made in writing so, and the choice that other poets made in writing differently. His choice was, as she says, 'to celebrate a mystery rather than to describe and comment upon an event'; and to celebrate it by 'great ancient images' rather than by local trope, sensuous detail and so on. It is good to be reminded (what is forgotten by dispensers of Poetry as the immediate instrument of social therapy) that some poems are cables not so much between the individual poet and reader as between the ancient world and our own, preserving—in a way that history books, and poems written in close engagement with either world, can't—continuity of apperception. But that continuity may be flimsy. My case is that the nativity tradition itself is not uniform; and Milton subsumes only about half of it in his Ode.

To take the authorities cited by Cook and Miss Tuve: Lactantius (d. 325), though an interesting writer, is in this case (*Institutes*, IV, V, etc.) merely an unimpressive particle of Augustine, heavily determined by circumstance: an anti-Platonist, a primitivist, a defender of the faith against persecution and against sex.

[1] 'The Study of Poetry'.

Vaughan: 'Incarnation and Passion', 'Christ's Nativity', 'Son-Days', 'The Shepherds', 'The Night'. Herrick: 'Christmas Caroll, sung to the King', 'The Star-Song', epigrams and some secular carols.

Mantuan's *Parthenice Mariana* (c. 1500) was an appropriate enough text for schoolboy Christian Humanists, 'non sine ingenio', as Scaliger remarked, 'sed sine arte'; the verse 'mollis, languidus, fluxus, incompositus, sine numeris, plebeius'.[1] Like the work of Macrobius, it has some interest as a compendium, but only the last book deals with the nativity and it is there that most of the flashes (realistic descriptions of winter and the birth of the child) and most of the parallels with Milton occur. The rest is mythology, moralizing and Marian lore. Sannazzaro's early sixteenth-century *De Partu Virginis* is an epyllion on the prophecy-nativity-crucifixion scheme so completely classical that it perverts the materials rather as Pre-Raphaelitism perverted the Middle Ages. Sannazzaro spent twenty years retouching it and won two titles—Christian Virgil and *Statarius Poeta.* The eighteenth-century divine who wrote a memoir of him found in the poem 'an air of *gentilism* strangely inconsistent with its subject' which 'in the opinion of some, rendered the motive of the author exceedingly questionable'. This is akin to Johnson on 'Lycidas'; but Ruskin too had things to say about that sort of religious art.[2]

Prudentius (fourth century) is more sympathetic. But his work shows up Milton's Ode as only partially traditional. Prudentius invented the ode of Christian devotion, but his nativity hymn, *Kalendas Ianuarius,* is more contemplative than Milton's, and unlike it in content (except for the already orthodox reference from Incarnation to Last Judgement, which Prudentius stresses more than Milton). His Epiphany hymn, cited as part of the tradition of idolatry's decay at the birth of Christ, has only eight out of 208 lines on the subject, and they are immediately followed by the last eight lines of the hymn, calling on all nations to rejoice that 'rex unus omnes possidet' and 'iam nemo posthac mortuus' because Christ lives. This is in the orthodox tradition of epiphany as the moment of revelation of Christ to the gentiles. Milton, typically, insets philosophical and political concerns between nativity and epiphany; and he presents the effect on paganism as ruin, not enlightenment. Prudentius has more about the decay of idolatry in *Apotheosis,* a Christological poem, but there the pagan deities

[1] 'Not without talent, but without art.' 'Soft, languid, relaxed, irregular, deficient in versification, vulgar.'

[2] *Modern Painters,* IV. iv, about the false ideal in religious art.

are dismissed in the reported speech of a topical anecdote about Julian the Apostate's revival of pagan rites (449 ff.); it is followed by a reference to the temple not made with hands (518) and a quotation of 'Verbum caro factum est' (525); Milton makes neither allusion. In *Kalendas Ianuarius* Prudentius uses two other motifs which Milton doesn't: the conceit of incarnation as a new spring, and the legend of beasts adoring Christ. The first—'vagitus ille exordium vernantis orbis prodidit'[1] (61–2)—has been grafted on to a quotation from Milton's Ode in Edwin Muir's 'The Christmas':

> Midnight strikes. One star awake
> Watches the Mother and the Child
> Who with his little hands will make
> Spring blossom in the winter wild.[2]

This makes Milton's omission of it—and of other naturalistic motifs—obvious. The conceit is thoroughly orthodox. It is based on a number of texts in *Isaiah*, especially chapter xxxv—e.g., 'The wilderness and the solitary place shall be glad for them; and the desert shall rejoice, and blossom as the rose'—along with references in *Psalms, Canticles* and *Revelation* to springing vegetation, water and other symbols of renewed vitality. It occurs in folk carols ('Sprung is the perfect May'), in Crashaw, and Herrick:

> Dark and dull night, fly hence away,
> And give the honour to this day,
> That sees December turned to May,
> ('Christmas Caroll')

It was still alive for Smart:

> Nature's decorations glisten
> Far above their usual trim;
> Birds on box and laurels listen,
> As so near the cherubs hymn.

1 'That crying child brought about the beginning of a springtime world.'

2 *One Foot in Eden* (1956).

Boreas now no longer winters
  On the desolated coast;
Oaks no more are riv'n in splinters
  By the whirlwind and his host.

Spinks and ouzles sing sublimely,
  'We too have a Saviour born,'
Whiter blossoms burst untimely
  On the blest Mosaic thorn.
            ('Nativity of Our Lord')

I am not suggesting that these poets[1] used the conceit, any more than Milton used an oblique reference to the *sol invictus* of Mithraism, to turn Christmas back into a solar festival; simply that here, in sources which Milton drew on for other items, was one which he did not use, and to which the atmosphere of his poem is alien.

Prudentius uses the legend of the beasts (*Kal. Ian.* 69–70, 80–84) most elaborately in *Apotheosis*. The birth of Christ, his power to destroy both pagan delusion and Judaic legalism, is celebrated by *natural* music—human song, including the echo of shepherds' voices in pastoral caves, and all the instruments of Bible story and psalm; this music (implicitly Orphean) quickens even dumb things to praise (386–92). The source is again *Isaiah*, e.g. 'The beast of the field shall honour me, the dragons and the owls' (xliii. 20), and 'the mountains and the hills shall break forth before you into singing, and all the trees of the field shall clap their hands' (lv. 12), together with similar motifs in the psalms: it is the typical, noble Hebrew expression of animism. More attention was (and is) paid to the detail of 'The ox knoweth his owner, and the ass his master's crib' (*Isa.* i. 3), but the larger-scale adoration had been handled already in the apocryphal *Gospel of Pseudo-Matthew* (xiv), by Dunbar in *Rorate coeli desuper*—'All fish in flood and fowl of flight Be mirthful and make melody'—and by Beaumont in *Psyche* (vii. 220). So in Milton's poem the shame, awe and obedience of Nature, wind and water, stars, and the legendary calm of the halcyons, are unusually submissive responses to the event.

[1] Except of course Muir, and accidentally in secular carols such as 'The holly and the ivy' and 'The twelve days of Christmas'.

The general differences between Milton and Prudentius correspond to these of detail. Milton at this stage was a platonizing Puritan in the uneasy last years of the Anglican settlement. Prudentius was an earnest evangel of a Christianity which, though it had not yet entirely superseded paganism, had recently attained imperial establishment. Although a violent anti-Platonist (e.g. *Apoth.* 200) and a strong Paulinist, he is on the winning side, seeing Christianity as the fulfilment of the classical world. Though much closer to practised idolatry, his emotions are not so engaged with it as Augustine's, or Milton's. He is therefore more genial. In his *Psychomachia*, Chastity's answer to Lust is more positive than the Lady's to Comus: Lust is defeated already by Christ's raising of the flesh to divinity at his incarnation (71 ff.).

The language of Milton's poetry is notoriously deficient in 'body'. His theories, in later life than the Ode, after his Platonic phase, ran to the Hebraic identification of soul with body, the dignity of the unfallen human frame, and the possibility that, without a Fall, man could have ascended the scale of being into an angelic state which he believed to be still corporeal, still sensory but more so—'Spirits that live throughout Vital in every part' (*P.L.* vi. 344). But for Milton this was a wished condition; he muddled it rather in the epic, and could not realize it verbally as Donne, another angelologist, despite his own dualism, occasionally did. Here in the Ode, though dealing with the occasion on which spirit became flesh, he is indifferent to most of the traditions that expressed joy in the perfecting of nature. He concentrates on those elements—peace, light, harmony—which lie at the nonhuman end of the spectrum. This 'spirituality' is not of the kind manifest, under personal pressure, in *The Doctrine and Discipline of Divorce* and some of his antiprelatical pamphlets: it is more Platonic than Pauline. And it is a spirituality which he does not see arriving *in* the infant. Prudentius understood the Pauline spirit and flesh, and saw what happened to them at the birth of Christ:

> Abraham saw God and straightway believed that he had seen him; but thou [Christ], who art his descendant after the flesh, seest all things after the manner of flesh, and performest the works of the flesh, under a law which is fulfilled only by the spirit within; nor is that law carnal which issued from heaven

and which thou dost fulfil in the flesh, but a law pregnant with Christ that should be delivered of my hope.

(*Apoth.* 367–72)

It is essentially a 'Metaphysical' apprehension. Jonson:

The Word, which heaven and earth did make
Was now laid in a manger

Donne:

Thou'hast light in darke; and shutst in little roome,
Immensity cloysterd in thy deare wombe.

Herbert:

O Thou, whose glorious, yet contracted light,
Wrapt in nights mantle, stole into a manger;
Since my dark soul and brutish is thy right,
To Man of all beasts be thou not a stranger:

Crashaw, classically epigrammatic:

Wellcome, all WONDER'S in one sight!
Æternity shutt in a span.
Sommer in Winter. Day in Night.
Heaven in earth, & GOD in MAN.
Great little one! whose all-embracing birth
Lifts earth to heaven, stoopes heav'n to earth.
('Nativity Hymn')

Even the neo-classical Drummond:

In a poor cottage inn'd a Virgin maid,
A weakling, did him bear who all upbears.

And, curiously the most comprehensive of this group, Beaumont:

The Day which made *Immensity* become
A *Little one*; which printed godly *May*
On pale *December's* face; which drew the *Sun*
Of *Paradise* into a *Bud*; the Day
Which shrunk *Eternity* into a *Span*
Of Time, Heav'n into *Earth, God* into *Man.*
(vii. 156)

These oxymorons, though an improvement on Fletcher's fluttering antitheses, do not express, only state the fundamental metaphor of

Christendom; but they try to, and, especially Herbert's, try within hearing of Shakespeare's pre-eminently 'incarnational' use of language. Vaughan, alone, achieved creative imagery, especially in 'The Night', a poem referring to Nicodemus' secret visit to Jesus and so to rebirth of the flesh by the spirit (*John*, iii):

Through that pure virgin shine,
    That sacred veil drawn o'er Thy glorious noon,
That men might look and live, as glow-worms shine,
        And face the moon:
    Wise Nicodemus saw such light
    As made him know his God by night.

        Most blest believer he!
Who in that land of darkness and blind eyes
Thy long-expected healing wings could see
        When thou didst rise!
    And, what can never more be done,
    Did at midnight speak with the Sun!

        O who will tell me, where
He found thee at that dead and silent hour?
What hallow'd solitary ground did bear
        So rare a flower;
    Within whose sacred leaves did lie
    The fulness of the Deity?

    No mercy-seat of gold,
No dead and dusty cherub, nor carv'd stone
But his own living works did my Lord hold
        And lodge alone;
    Where trees and birds did watch and peep
    And wonder, while the Jews did sleep.

It is not a question of original 'ideas': Vaughan is steeped in the tradition. His verses constantly paraphrase the prophets and gospels; the cloud, the veil, the trees and birds are traditional carol motifs; the typology of sun-son, incarnation-resurrection, the Mary-rose emblem, are orthodox. In his poem about 'The Shepherds' Vaughan glances at Melchisidech's Salem in a neo-Latin way, but 'Her cedar, fir, hew'd stones and gold' are passed over in favour of Bethelehem's thatch. This is a case of the association (implicit ground of much criticism today) of classicism with an aristocratic culture, and Metaphysical poetry with democracy.

Milton does not attempt the grand paradox. His only reference to incarnation as such is:

And here with us to be,
Forsook the Courts of everlasting Day,
And chose with us a darksom House of mortal Clay.

Philanthropic assumption of a disguise is true to neither the synoptic gospel and medieval carol tradition of the blessed babe, nor the Johannine *verbum caro factum est*. The metaphor's theatricality is paralleled in 'The Passion':

He sovran Priest stooping his regal head
That dropd with odorous oil down his fair eyes,
Poor fleshly Tabernacle entered,
His starry front low-rooft beneath the skies;
O what a mask was there, what a disguise!

The nativity references in *Paradise Lost* XII (240, 324, 360, 379) and *Regained* I (86, 130, 234—repetition of *P.L.* XII. 360) are of the same kind but even thinner, as their context is; all (not only, as might be expected, Satan's at *P.R.* I. 86) put the paradox, as Ode and 'Passion' do, in *political* terms—'For know, thou art no Son of mortal man, / Though men esteem thee low of Parentage, / Thy Father is the Eternal King'. So at the end of the Ode the babe is cleverly restored to the courts of everlasting day:

Heav'ns youngest teemed Star,
Hath fixt her polisht Car,
Her sleeping Lord with Handmaid Lamp attending:
And all about the Courtly Stable,
Bright-harnest Angels sit in order serviceable.

This avoids his immediate destiny. Accordingly, the fine reference to his destiny in stanza xvi—

The Babe lies yet in smiling Infancy,
That on the bitter cross
Must redeem our loss;
So both himself and us to glorifie:

—is overwhelmed by an epical description of the last judgement which, Milton says, must occur before that glorification. This denies all the New Testament claims that incarnation and crucifixion have already effectively sanctified the flesh, fulfilled the law, and punished sin in those who believe. The majority of medieval carols (e.g. 'This endrys nyȝt') use the 'second Adam' theme, and link nativity to crucifixion, much more richly than Milton does.

The only beings actually to come down to earth in Milton's Ode are Peace, and, in the future, Mercy supported by Truth and Justice. To personify abstractions in order to affirm incarnation is to apply the definitive resources of language to shadow forth the visual arts. *Ut pictura poesis* was a respected theory; but not all poets obeyed it, and Milton, in obeying it, was obeying a dictate of temperament as well as art. The notion of Nature hiding her guilty front with innocent snow at the descent of Peace may be an allegorical type of the judgement of Adam and Eve; but I have been able to find it only in the apocryphal *Revelation of St. John the Theologian*. The hysterical nature of this work—which also concentrates on putting the evil spirits to flight—confirms a suspicion that in these stanzas Milton, faced with the rude fact of a god being born, is confused and falls (as in the last stanza but one) into the worst kind of imagery—personification which is extremely figurative but not in the least natural. It allows us to see through the myth to the skeleton of incest anxiety; and, knowing Milton, we may also see the lines as an exorcism of his recent *In adventum veris* (*On the Coming of Spring*):

> Rejuvenated Earth discards despised old age and yearns for the Sun's embrace: yearns, and is worthy too, for what more beautiful than Earth when she voluptuously bares her all-succouring breasts that breathe the balm of Araby, and from her lovely lips distils sweet spices and the rose of Venus? (55)

The coyness of 'the little hyperbolical fiction' Miss Tuve admits (p. 49); but it is not, as she claims, justified by any significant use of 'the ancient figure of the fertilizing intercourse between earth and sky' (p. 50). This 'figure', the image of heavenly rain or dew, is linked with the December-May motif discussed above. It starts in *Isaiah*: 'the parched ground shall become a pool, and the thirsty land springs of water (xxxv. 7) . . . Drop down, ye heavens, from above, and let the skies pour down righteousness: let the earth open, and let them bring forth salvation, and let righteousness spring up together; I Yahveh have created it (xlv. 8) . . . For as the rain cometh down, and the snow from heaven, and returneth not thither, but watereth the earth, and maketh it bring forth and bud, that it may give seed to the sower, and bread to the eater, so shall my word be that goeth forth out of my mouth (lv. 10) . . . For as the earth bringeth forth her bud, and as the garden causeth the things that are sown in it to spring forth; so the Lord God will cause righteousness and praise to spring forth before all the nations' (lxi. 11). These references, and similar ones in *Psalms* and *Song of Solomon*, had been taken up before, crudely in Dunbar's *Rorate coeli desuper*, naturalistically in 'I syng of a mayden':

He cam also stylle
Þere his moder was
As dew in Aprylle
    Þat fallyt on þe gras;
He cam also stylle
    To his moderes bowr
As dew in Aprille
    Þat fallyt on þe flour;
He cam also stylle
    Þere his moder lay
As dew in Aprille
    Þat fallyt on þe spray;

This carol's immediate text is *Psalm* lxxii: 'He shall come down like rain upon the mown grass: as showers that water the earth'. That is also a psalm about peace (though not, it happens, proper to any holy day); but it is peace especially for 'the poor of the people' and 'the children of the needy'. In *Isaiah* xi, proper lesson for the second Sunday in Advent, this merciful government is wonderfully associated with the peace of nature and with intuitive righteousness; and it is seen as stemming physically from Jesse:

> And there shall come a rod out of the stem of Jesse, and a Branch shall grow out of his roots: And the spirit of Yahveh shall rest upon him . . . and shall make him of quick understanding in the fear of Yahveh . . . with righteousness shall he judge the poor, and [plead] with equity for the meek of the earth: and he shall smite the earth with the rod of his mouth . . .

The wolf also shall dwell with the lamb . . . and a little child shall lead them.

Prudentius incorporated this text in *Hymnus Epiphaniae* (49). It was anglicized in the fifteenth-century carol 'At Cristemasse, mayde Mary':

Þan myȝt þe mylde may singe,
    Ysaye, þe woord of þee:
'Þou seydest a ȝerd schulde sprynge
    Oute of þe rote of jentill Jesse,
And schulde floure with florisschyng,
    With primeroses greet plente;
Into þe croppe schulde come a Kyng   (top branch)
    Þat is a Lord of power and pyte—
    My swete Sone I see!
I am þe ȝerde, þou art þe Flour!
My Brid is borne by beest in boure;
My Primerose, my Paramour,
    With love I lulle þee.

And Smart was to relate it to the justice of the third proper psalm for Christmas Day, lxxxv:

Thy truth and mercy for increase
    Of love have met in bliss,
Stern righteousness and gentle peace
    Have join'd the holy kiss.
From Christ the branch fair truth shall sprout
    And bloom again on earth,
And justifying grace come out
    From heav'n at Shilo's birth.
(*Psalms of David*)

I am not claiming virtue for the particularization of Smart's 'sprout', but I am suggesting that the scriptural insight which prompted him to evangelize the psalms was superior to Milton's, and that the direction Milton takes in his poem—and, traditionally, need not have taken—is away from the incarnate towards the ideate.

The second descent, of Mercy, Truth and Justice, has only the abstract effect of a reference to eschatology, because Milton is thinking of political rather than spiritual qualities. This descent is authorized (as Miss Tuve notes) by proper psalms for Christmas and St. Stephen's Day. But *Psalm* lxxxv offers one element of the apotheosis in the present tense, another in erotic imagery, and the third in natural metaphor: mercy and truth *are* met together, righteousness and peace have *kissed*, 'Truth shall spring out of the earth; and righteousness shall look down from heaven'. When he translated this psalm Milton (unlike Smart) trivially cadenced and visualized the imagery of these lines. In the Ode he transmutes them into a baroque fresco of the kind in which angels appear to be descending feet-foremost from the pink-clouded centre of a vault. Miss Tuve won't allow that this is *icon*. But if it is not painting it is, certainly, masque. In Jonson's *Golden Age Restored* (1615), Astrea and the Golden Age descend in just this way while Pallas Athene, the presenter, invokes them with the conceit that Milton had inherited from Sannazzaro and he from Virgil:

> Descend, you long, long wished and wanted pair,
> And as your softer times *divide* the air,
> So take all clouds off with your golden hair.[1]

That Milton should have handled the psalm in the same way in his poem must disconcert any modern reader who values either.[2] We may excuse and understand: the phantasy is appropriate to the perfect bliss not yet to be, especially in contrast to the purely linguistic effect of the next stanza, 'The Babe lies yet in smiling Infancy, / That on the bitter cross / Must redeem our loss'; masque was familiar, and often moralistic; Astraea was equated with Virgo in the zodiac, so Milton's Justice illustrates the Virgin. But I doubt if we can accept it completely: it seems to offend a more than temporary principle of decorum. Jonson's masque is

[1] Cf. 'the amorous clouds dividing'; Sannazzaro uses the conceit for describing Mercury at I. 83 and 90. It is in these discordant stanzas that Milton is closest to Latin verse composition. 'Pollute with sinful blame': *pollutus*. 'She strikes a universall Peace through Sea and Land': classical and patristic authors of the *pax romana, passim*; Sannazzaro, 'Interea terra pacta iam pace marique' (II. 116); Mantuan, 'Iam mare, iam tellus italo perterrita marte Caesaris imperium . . . Pax erat'.

[2] Not that the psalm is actually about the nativity. If we take over the scriptural interpretation of an earlier age, especially its typology, wholesale, what we gain in understanding that age's literature may cost a continued misunderstanding of the Bible in our own. See *Literature and Dogma*.

all masque, and consistently allegorical, classical, and political—the Iron Age calling forth the Evils in defiance of prophecy, dancing an antimasque to 'a confusion of martial music' and being turned to stone by Pallas' wand. (Even so, it concludes with a dance to celebrate the restored innocence of erotic love, with which Jonson—more perceptively than Milton at this age—associated honest government.) Again, we are being accustomed to the Renaissance habit of emblematic pagan-Christian eclecticism (scholarship on the Neoplatonists, and the pagan mysteries, etc.). But the question is one of value, and of relation between the traditional habit and the individual genius. In this case, the masque-like stanza indicates the direction of Milton's poem as a whole—theoretical, ornate: the babe is to become Mercy at the judgement day, realizing then the furniture of the ark. But it is only that eschatological half of the paradox that Milton realizes in his poem: what the babe is now, and will be to men in secular time, he omits. Whenever things descend, Milton accoutres them with those very furnishings which another tradition took to have been laid aside by Christ; Vaughan did away with them—'No mercy-seat of gold, No dead and dusty cherub, nor carv'd stone . . .'

There is a third descent in stanza viii, when Christ himself does arrive, but hypothetically and allegorically, as Pan. Annotation makes the introduction of Pan significant: in Macrobius, for instance, he was identified with the sun who has just been dismissed; he was in love with Echo, representing the harmony of the spheres, and their inaccessibility to mortal sensation; in a tradition summarized in the notes to May in the *Shepheardes Calender* he was the Good Shepherd; and by a false etymology his name stood for ubiquitousness and omnipotence. It would be silly to reject annotations of this kind, and to condemn poetry which subsumes them. But here the poem does not support their weight, or the weight of its own pun, 'kindly [naturally] com to live with them below'. Vaughan takes the allusion further, to

> their souls' Great Shepherd, Who was come
> To bring all stragglers home;
> Where now they find Him out, and, taught before,
> That Lamb of God adore,
>
> ('The Shepherds')

Milton, as Miss Tuve says, 'makes much of the fact that "nature" does not understand the Incarnation. We are shown it by one figure after another—stars, sun, shepherds, *natura*' (p. 51). Vaughan makes much of another 'fact', that the shepherds and they alone did understand: 'How happen'd it that in the dead of night / You only saw true light?' Beaumont exalts his shepherds almost to translation for having first seen the light (vii. 220). Again Milton's choice of tradition lies far away from that apprehension of Christ represented by the *Secunda Pastorum*. (At the same time he minimises those connotations of Pan which are heroic; and the Herculean reference in stanza xxv—the only point at which the dispersion of idolatry is attributed directly to the infant—is left slight.)

Finally, Milton alone, even among classical and patristic authors, ignores the central naturalness of motherhood. Mantuan and Sannazzaro watch the baby being born, feel the body's warmth, see him at the breast:

> Candida formosae iam pendet ad ubera matris:
> Infantem fovet ipsa sinu:
>
> Tunc Puerum repido Genitrix involvit amictu,
> Exceptumque sinu, blandeque ad pectora pressum
> Detulit in praesepe.[1]
>
> (*De Part. Virg.* ii. 377)

The oxymorons of Milton's poem—'Wherein the Son of Heav'ns Eternal King, Of Wedded Maid and Virgin Mother born'—avoid the flesh, limiting the event to its theologic formulation. Even the theology is politically partial: it does not approach the Hellenistic spirituality of *John*, nor realize the extraordinary psychology of *Isaiah* liv: 'For thy Maker is thine husband'. Donne offers an inkling of how the nativity soothes even Oedipean anxiety:

> Ere by the spheares time was created, thou
> Wast in his minde, who is thy Sonne, and Brother;
> Whom thou conceiv'st, conceiv'd; yea thou art now
> Thy Makers maker, and thy Father's mother;
>
> ('Annunciation')

Innocence is not elicited from experience in Milton's Ode.

[1] 'Now he hangs at the white breasts of his lovely mother: She warms him in her very bosom.' 'Then the Mother wraps the Child in a mantle, catches him up and gently presses him to her breast; then she puts him into his crib.'

What Milton does positively celebrate is the counterpart of what he avoids. It is the quasi-Platonic principles of peace as an effect of that night (stanzas iv–v) and harmony as a symbol of cosmic order (xi–xiii) which are linguistically perfected in the poem. They are so fully realized as to need no annotative support from tradition. Yet they subsume enlightening allusions—to mention only three not remarked on elsewhere. In 'And Kings sate still with awful eye, As if they surely knew their sovran Lord was by', the epithet 'sovran' points the oxymoron of healing might. The halcyons, recalling the brooding Spirit of *Genesis* i, indicate what stanza xii makes explicit, that the incarnation is a second creation, on the authority of *Isaiah* xlv and *John* i. 'Ring out ye Chrystall Sphears' makes the bells of Christmas morning chime in eternity, and makes them signify a more than birthday joy. Now, the peace and harmony and light realize, with typically Miltonic solidity and force, what is an ideate condition: an architectural world founded in chaos, harmony metallically rung out of discord, the gleaming angels vertical against a globe of light in the midst of uncomprehending darkness. And fading as the true light begins to shine are the abuses of idolatry's half-light, deceptive beauty, usurping power. These need no annotation either: even if we don't know who Libyc Hammon is, the shrinking of his horn tells us, along with the Tyrian maids, that a false phallicism is collapsing; and there are some bold allusive indications here too, such as '*Ashtaroth*, / Heav'ns Queen and Mother both'.

But what is the nexus between the defeated fear and lust, and the victorious peace and harmony? It is not the babe in the stable. It seems intended to be (as in the Latin analogues) the salvific *policy* implicit in the proem and in stanzas xv–xviii (such an aggrandisement of the domestic being typical of Christian Humanism). But this theoretical connection is not felt in the hymn so strongly as the two climaxes of the greater sun and the dragon. The marvellously skilled phonetic hushing of the hymn's first six stanzas culminates in a moment not in any usual sense incarnational—

He saw a greater Sun appear
Then his bright Throne or burning Axletree could bear.

—but one that makes of that lowly birth a cosmic victory over natural power. The binding of the dragon's swingeing tail is of similar though more directly psychological import. These are the poem's hinges. Symbolizing the conquest by hard-edged right reason of the soft dim liquid allures of passion, they make the poem Miltonic, and relate it more closely to his other poems than to prophets, gospels or analogues: the same dark illusions are defeated in *Comus*, the same weltering waves and tangled hair of nymphs are transcended in 'Lycidas', the same mystical rays of solid light dazzle error in the prose and *Paradise Lost*, the same gigantic force ruins idolatry in *Samson*. In the Ode, of course, the poet's power to synthesize and reconcile, and to purge, is offered implicitly as a symbol of Christ's redeeming power. But that is to suggest that Christ's was a Miltonic victory, not of transformation (as trope would symbolize), or of love over law, but of arrangement: a schematic conquest. The poem's active power has a dual sanction: the art which establishes peace and enacts harmony in stanzas iv–v, xii–xiii, and the intellectual force which in those stanzas amalgamates *Isaiah* with the *pax romana, Job* with the *Timaeus*. The art—pre-eminently an art of cosmic control and comprehension—is astonishing. 'And all the spangled host keep watch in squadrons bright' suspends the sun as God did for Joshua on Gibeon. 'See how from far upon the Eastern rode' fixes a vast aesthetic distance. The aspirates and *o*'s of stanza x make the whole world echo. But when we come to the idols we see (especially when we refer to the tradition) that they are being defeated by this art rather than by Christ. The mutters, shrieks and weeping of stanzas xix–xxi set themselves plainly enough against the eloquent music of ix–xiii: they are not silenced by the Word. Art makes the gods of Nile hideously brutish in themselves, but there is no divinely human counterpart. The blue flames of Moloch, the timbrelled darkness of Osiris, present an essentially aesthetic, not a moral contrast with the herald angels' glittering ranks. The whole section is prosodically unified, by the repeated 'vain'; the repetition of [ɔ] in 'O're, shore, haunted, torn, mourn, horn, mourn, nor, naught, sorcerers' and [aʊ] in 'unshowr'd, profoundest, shroud', etc.; and the cadences of the alexandrines contrast with their firmness in the earlier stanzas. It is not enough that the qualities so ascribed to the idols—darkness and so on—derive moral significance from biblical usage: in the Bible, God is always present, acting on them; here they are caught into a pattern of art which de-moralizes the materials.

To this objection, that the sanction of the poem's action is not divine power but Miltonic art and intellect, there are three answers: (1) The Ode is not meant to be a Metaphysical contemplation but a hymn of praise; (2) The art of the hymn is dedicated by the proem; (3) Art is in any case a manifestation of the divine in man.

(1) and (2). Yes, but notions of hymnic decorum didn't prevent David and Petronius and Smart, Mary, Zacharias and Simeon (*Luke* i–ii) from moving more easily than Milton does between the physical symbols of parturition and the abstract of light and dark, or from making it clear that the power belonged to God. Miss Tuve claims that 'A hymn is not only a "praise", but usually a liturgical act of praise, by definition usually written as Sidney says "*to imitate the inconceivable* excellencies of God"' (p. 42). Her italics beg the question of the Ode's Platonizing tendency, because Sidney was trying to beg it too by turning the tables on Plato with his own Christian Platonism and on the Puritans with the usual gesture at the psalms. The ethnocentricity of his Platonic reading of the psalms (but also his appreciation of their joy in the natural world) is apparent when he says David's imagery makes you 'as it were, see God comming in his Maiestie; his telling of the Beastes joyfulnes, and hills leaping . . . a heuenlie poesie, wherein almost hee sheweth himselfe a passionate louer of that vnspeakable and euerlasting beautie to be seene by the eyes of the minde, onely cleered by fayth'. The beatific vision is not really an element in the Bible and it was only temporarily an element in English religious literature. Further, Milton's Ode is not liturgical in any way in which the *Benedicite* (and his own paraphrase of it at *P.L.* V. 153), *Benedictus, Cantate Domino, Magnificat* or *Nunc Dimittis* are: it lacks their comprehensiveness and unity, and their dedicated generosity. The obvious criterion is Smart's *Song to David*—rhetorical, book-learned, esoteric, unique yet not in the disabling sense personal, for there is an impelling tension between the poet and his materials as between his enthusiasm and his late-Augustan diction. Significantly, it is Smart who, alone in his century, could combine a sense of the traditional typology with a Metaphysical insight into incarnation:

> God all-bounteous, all-creative,
>   Whom no ills from good dissuade,

Is incarnate, and a native
Of the very world he made.

Milton's hymn is something given, but something Milton has constructed himself rather than, in the hymnic way, an act of praise celebrating what God has done. His dating of the poem even suggests he wanted to give it to himself as a coming-of-age present. As the superb pomp of the induction's organ shows, it isn't really any less egotistical than Milton's other poems. My point is that we must not accept it simply as part of 'the tradition': being so Miltonic, it must be regarded in the light of his other work; sharing so much of learned, Platonizing Christian Humanism's partial apperception of the gospel, its ethos has to be completed by the intuitions of carol and Metaphysical devotion.

For (3), it is only at certain periods that this *kind* of art—the technical will, instrument of rationality trained to vanquish the lusts of the flesh and impose an ideal order on the world—has corresponded to notions of the divine, or symbolized an ethic held to be pre-eminently useful in the conduct of life. We may prefer some less anxiously arrogant art, in which nature has more play, and spirit is less Platonic: an art, and an ethic, empirically closer to the facts of life. Readers' predispositions prevent agreement about this; indeed, the arguments here presented on either side themselves result from an over-anxiously moral preoccupation with the moral content of poetry—on one side, too faithful respect for allusive orthodoxy, on the other too credulous valuation of verbalized naturalness. But this kind of philosophical dichotomizing is what we're driven to by the poem's art: we can't 'do' anything with the art, only experience it. This ode is distinguished within the tradition and (along with 'Lycidas', 'At a Solemn Musick' and *Comus*) within Milton's *oeuvre*, by its artistry. It is superior to its Latin analogues in the same way as it is superior to *In quintum Novembris* and different from the epics: instead of a theme being lengthened into narrative and expanded with speeches, descriptions and didactics, an invented lyric form carries a sustained vocal impulse and a scheme of references which concentrate theme, legend and sermon into a fugue or mosaic of elementary sounds and primary colours. Although reading a 'musical' poem isn't in the least like listening to music, we have some idea what we mean by this. We haven't, though, any idea what the effect of such 'artful recitations', however 'sweetened with graceful enticements to the love and practice of justice, temperance, and fortitude', may be. So we have to talk about what is said, or who said it. If we talk at all it is in spite of Milton: as with all his poems, he deliberately and suddenly relinquishes it —'Time is our tedious Song should here have ending'—to our contemplation as artifact. That he does so, and that he habitually makes so much more than conventional efforts at invocation and dedication, suggest he had difficulty in delivering his work from personality enough for it to be viable. His poems feel like acts. This distinguishes them from most Metaphysical poems: Milton's symbolize works rather than faith. So they do not engage us in a mesh of emotional apprehension. The Ode does not admit 'The uncontrollable mystery on the bestial floor': partly because Milton associated the animal with sin, and mystery with chaos; but also because he was a magus determined to control the mystery. So we lose the persuasive reverence of Metaphysical poetry, and the reflective investigations of mythological sonnets. What we finally gain, beyond the incalculable gains of mere art, is, from that struggled objectivity, a malely respectful freedom, to do —as we are assumed able to do—what we will with the poem; and, in spite of it, an insight into what such an imperious treatment of experience as Milton's may involve: that is where we move back into morality again with the unfair, subjectively-answered but irresistible question, 'What, consistently, would be the concomitants of a life whose energies were directed as they symbolically are in this poem?'

III

APPROACHES TO *LYCIDAS*

G. S. Fraser

I

WHEN YOUNG students of English, without a classical education, today first come across *Lycidas*, it often strikes them as a poem of a dauntingly unfamiliar kind. That was my own experience as a schoolboy, and I thought that Milton might well have invented the kind. In fact it is a poem set so firmly in a tradition that John Crowe Ransom has described it as 'a poem nearly anonymous'. The tradition is that of the pastoral elegy. The pastoral elegy had its roots in the Alexandrian or earlier Hellenistic period of the ancient world (roughly in the third and second centuries before Christ). From its beginnings, it was an extremely literary and sophisticated kind of poem, especially sophisticated in its imitations of naïvety. Theocritus and Bion and Moschus, like Milton himself, though they wrote about shepherds and rustic life, were either born in or passed a good deal of time in towns. Like Milton, they were extremely literate. The pastoral elegy, both in the ancient world and in the Renaissance when the form acquired a revived popularity, was written about shepherds, but never by them; and from the beginning shepherds were always essentially a way of talking about something else (about poets, for instance), with metaphorical indirection. The shepherds, besides being poets, might in Milton's time be courtiers or lovers or parsons (because a parson is a pastor, and his congregation are his flock), and they could discuss in doric allegory a very wide range of topics, including topics tricky or dangerous to discuss directly, such as politics, theology, church government. Like the pageants and entertainments of the Elizabethan period, they could criticize the current state of affairs in a manner which was both sanctioned by authority and gave some outlet for popular feeling.

The pastoral elegy was ceasing to be a centrally fashionable form when Milton wrote *Lycidas*. As a Cambridge poet (he had taken his degree about five years ago, and was living in the country, devoting himself to the monumental private studies and the self-disciplining which he considered prerequisites for the making of a great poet), Milton was asked to contribute to a volume of elegies for his fellow-student, Edward King, drowned in the Irish Channel in 1637. Collections of elegies, like collections of panegyrics or prefatory verses, were common in the earlier seventeenth century, and reflected the poet's sense of one of his functions in an ordered community. Milton, in *Lycidas*, was harking back to Spenser, whereas the most fashionable poet who contributed to King's memorial volume, Cleveland, was a neo-Donneian; rather in the sense in which Mr. John Wain and Mr. Alfred Alvarez were once described as neo-Empsonians.

We do not now read, unless we are scholars, much Renaissance pastoral poetry, apart from short lyrics like Marlowe's 'Come live with me and be my love'; though there are strong pastoral elements in some of Shakespeare's comedies, like *As You Like It*. We tend to think the pure pastoral convention artificial and boring, and have a very inadequate idea of its range. Thus we miss something (Miss Tuve makes this point) in *Lycidas* which must have been vividly present for contemporary readers, the echoes, the recognition of a family face. The echoes of Spenser's *Shepheardes Calender* (apart from the wider echoes of the whole extant body of pastoral poetry) are surprisingly close. Milton himself has left on record the particularly intimate nature of his debt to Spenser, 'a better teacher than . . . Aquinas', and Dryden noted that Spenser, Fairfax, and Milton form a single poetic family. The lovely turn at the end of *Lycidas*.

> Weep no more, woeful Shepherds, weep no more,

is very closely modelled on a similar turn at the end of Spenser's November eclogue in *The Shepheardes Calender*, and we can even find the good line of Spenser's out of which that great line of Milton's came:

Cease now my Muse, now cease thy sorrowes sourse . . .

We can find earlier in the same eclogue that plangent phrase, 'no more', which Milton loved so much:

Nymphs and Shepherds dance no more
By sandy *Ladons* Lilied banks,

though Spenser exploits its plangency in, compared to Milton, a clumsy way:

Matter of myrth now shalt thou have no more;
For dead is she, that myrth made thee of yore. . . .

The Shepheardes Calender is not, for most of us today, easy reading; when I did it as a set-book in the English course at St. Andrews a quarter of a century ago, I thought it was a kind of text a devilish professor might concoct for the sole purpose of tormenting undergraduates; and in fact Spenser largely conceived it as a text-book of poetic rhetoric, a book of working examples. It is written in an amateurish imitation of the style and spelling of medieval English poetry. Bits of dialect are dabbed on, and there is a pervading mock-rusticity that sometimes seems in a bad sense genuinely rustic (a clownish imitation of clownishness). E.K.'s notes at the end are likely to seem to a modern reader narrowly and drily technical. There is a lack of ordinary human interest, at least for us: Queen Elizabeth is flattered as queen of all the shepherds, swains argue for and against a Puritan view of Church government, and even the expression of personal grief, as in the eleventh eclogue, is very much in fancy dress. But go back to these poems of Spenser's from *Lycidas*, which owes so much to them, and you will begin to see more sympathetically what Spenser was after; at any rate, for Milton, he was good to steal from.

The flower catalogue was a stock feature of the pastoral elegy, and was associated with ideas of surviving fame, memorial tribute, and the possibility of resurrection. But Milton's catalogue of flowers in *Lycidas* derives very particularly from Spenser's catalogue in his April eclogue. It may be useful to set the two passages side by side: Milton's passage,

Bring the rathe Primrose that forsaken dies,
The tufted Crow-toe, and pale Gessamine,

The white Pink, and the Pansie freak't with jet,
The glowing Violet,
The Musk-rose, and the well attir'd Woodbine,
With Cowslips wan that hang the pensive hed,
And every flowr that sad embroidery wears:
Bid *Amarantus* all his beauty shed,
And Daffadillies fill their cups with tears,
To strew the Laureat Herse where *Lycid* lies,

alongside Spenser's passage,

'Bring hether the pincke and purple cullambine,
    'With gelliflowres;
'Bring coronations, and sops in wine,
    'Worn of paramoures:
'Strowe me the ground with daffadowndillies,
'And cowslips, and kingcups, and loved lillies;
    'The pretty pawnce,
    'And the chevisaunce,
'Shall match with the fayre flowre Delice.'

Sir Henry Wotton, in a commendatory letter prefacing *Comus*, compliments Milton on 'a certain Dorique delicacy in your Songs and Odes, wherunto I must plainly confess to have seen yet nothing parallel in our Language: *Ipsa mollities*'. These two passages perhaps illustrate what Wotton meant. Spenser seems to me here much more genuinely Doric than Milton but certainly, if in a way more robust, he is less delicate. Milton would have instinctively avoided the bouncy stress rhythms of

'Strowe me the ground with daffadowndillies,
'And cowslips, and kingcups, and loved lillies,'

which is genuinely Doric in the effect it gives of a puppy bounding about, at once clumsy and graceful. Milton is never whole-heartedly Doric in this way.

Yet he is following Spenser pretty carefully. Spenser's vivid descriptive word for a flower, 'sops in wine' is matched by Milton's 'Crow-toe': (these were the ordinary names for the flowers, but have a vivid country flavour); Spenser's 'daffadown-dillies' is matched by Milton's 'Daffadillies', where Shakespeare, Ben Jonson, and Herrick all write of 'daffodils'. Milton, also, rhymes 'Gessamine' with 'Woodbine' because Spenser has rhymed 'cullambine' with 'sops in wine'. The one phrase which has not a parallel in Spenser is the 'Pansy freak't with jet': John Ruskin thought this phrase a blot on the passage because of its undue particularization. He was thinking partly of Dr. Johnson's maxim about how the poet should generalize, not 'number the streaks of the tulip', and partly of decorum: does a swain observe things in this sort of detail? But all pansies are freaked with jet and we cannot be certain whether or not this phrase would have struck Milton's contemporaries as un-Dorically particular.

There are other debts in *Lycidas* to Spenser. Spenser's fifth eclogue is a dialogue about the wickedness of the Church of Rome, and contains these lines:

> Tho, under colour of shepheards, somewhile
> There crept in wolves, full of fraud and guile,
> That often devoured their own sheepe,
> And often the shepheards that did hem keep . . .

Milton borrowed the forcible verb 'crept' for Saint Peter's or Christ's (critics are not wholly agreed about which the pilot of the Galilean lake is) attack on unworthy Anglican clergymen:

> 'How well could I have spar'd for thee, young swain,
> 'Anow of such as for their bellies sake,
> 'Creep and intrude and climb into the fold?'

and later he makes a much more dramatic use than Spenser of Spenser's wolves:

> 'Besides what the grim Wolf with privy paw
> 'Daily devours apace, and nothing sed . . .'

Even closer than these Spenserian borrowings, however, is a borrowing from a poet more nearly contemporary with Milton, the neo-Spenserian Phineas Fletcher, the author of the long allegory about the human body as microcosm, *The Purple Island*. Fletcher also wrote pastorals. The quiet close of *Lycidas* is one of its triumphs:

> Thus sang the uncouth Swain to th'oaks and rills
> While the still morn went out with Sandals gray;
> He touchd the tender stops of various Quills,

With eager thought warbling his *Doric* lay:
And now the Sun had stretcht out all the hills,
And now was dropt into the Western bay;
At last he rose, and twitchd his Mantle blew:
Tomorrow to fresh Woods and Pastures new.

Here is the passage by Fletcher which that passage, obviously, was very closely modelled on:

But see, the stealing night with softly pace,
To flie the western sunne, creeps up the east;
Cold Hesper 'gins unmask his evening face,
And calls the winking stars from drouzie rest:
Home then my lambes; the falling drops eschew;
Tomorrow shall ye feast in pastures new,
And with the rising sun banquet on pearled dew.

Each of these passages exhibits a similar structure of events: sunset; the shepherd getting his sheep back to fold (implied, not stated, in Milton); and the shepherd deciding to move on to uncropped meadows in the morning. There is even the very striking coincidence of

Tomorrow to fresh woods and pastures new.

with Fletcher's

Tomorrow shall ye feast in pastures new.

But the most surprising resemblance is a much broader one; the tone, mood, and pace of Fletcher's passage are very like Milton, and indeed one would have said (if Fletcher hadn't written his passage first) typically Miltonic. Milton, also, on the whole improves on Spenser in his borrowings, but the Fletcher passage strikes me as being quite as well written as the Milton one, and tenderer:

Home then my lambes; the falling drops eschew. . . .

Quite as well written, that is, except for its last line: the phrase 'banquet on pearled dew', applied to sheep grazing early morning grass, strikes me as a breach of decorum; sheep know nothing about banquets or pearls, and shepherds not much. On the other hand, 'banquet' may here have its old sense of 'partake of refreshment'; and dew does look like pearls; at that level the phrase is defensible.

The closeness with which Milton follows Fletcher here forces us to grapple at last with that notion of John Crowe Ransom's with which we started: the notion of *Lycidas* as 'a poem nearly anonymous'. Milton in his later poetry is the most individual of all English poets, utterly unlike anyone else. Is he quite so individual in a comparatively early poem like *Lycidas*? Or is he trying to write a poem that anyone might have written, to sink himself completely in the pastoral tradition? Professor Fredson Bowers has pointed out that an argument against Mr. Ransom's theory could be based on the corrected manuscript of *Lycidas*, which is extant. If Mr. Ransom were right, all the alterations in this manuscript ought to be in the direction of Doric or, more broadly, of a typically homely pastoral diction; in fact, the most striking alterations are in an opposite direction.

Remarks on the diction of poems written more than three hundred years ago, when the spoken language was so different from what it is today, are likely to have a strong subjective flavour, especially when one is trying to point out very delicate distinctions of tone; and I do not write as an expert on the history of language, even of poetic language. But using one's vague sense of what a Doric or homely diction in pastoral was meant to be, in Fletcher's passage, for instance, ''gins unmask' and 'with softly pace' strike me as Doric or homely. ''Gins' has an archaic effect; 'softly' for 'soft' creates an effect of rustic confusion. Clearly, the Doric of pastoral was a highly artificial language, a compound of rustic words, archaic words, ordinary words used with an effect of deliberate simplicity and sometimes coined words used for an effect of quaintness. Milton, in one at least of his most important revisions of *Lycidas*, strikes me as ironing out the Doric.

One of the most moving passages in *Lycidas* feast read thus:

> what could the golden hayrd Calliope
> For her inchaunting son,
> When shee beheld (the gods farre sighted bee)
> His goarie scalp rowle downe the Thracian lee?

The little sentence in brackets, there, is Doric, or sophisticatedly naïve: 'be' for 'are' sounds rustic, plebeian, or archaic; but, more especially, it is sophisticatedly naïve, it is very much in the *persona* of an uncouth swain, to tell us that the gods are far-sighted: we knew this already. In his final rehandling of the passage Milton speaks not as the uncouth swain, but as himself, in his grandest style:

> What could the Muse herself that *Orpheus* bore,
> The Muse herself, for her inchanting son
> Whom Universal nature did lament,
> When, by the rout that made the hideous roar
> His goary visage down the stream was sent,
> Down the swift *Hebrus* to the *Lesbian* shore?

All the splendid alterations there are anti-Doric, directed against a style 'nearly anonymous'. The language of swains is vivid and concrete; it is more natural for them to speak of 'golden-haired Calliope' than to use an allusive and weighted term like 'the Muse'. They prefer images to concepts; they would not say 'Universal nature', but rather 'Great Pan'. It was a happy thought, too, of Milton's to get rid of the all too concrete gory scalp rolling (like a football) down the lea; but the gory visage—*visage*, so much more vague and so much more dignified than *scalp*—is, by comparison, as it is sent down the stream, unswainish; and the grand music of proper names in the last line is pure Milton and nobody else. In his revisions of this key passage, Milton is obviously aiming not at sinking himself in any anonymous style but at extreme elevation and individuality, at the Miltonic 'sublime': aiming at it, and hitting. And these considerations, taken all together, seem to put out of court the notion of *Lycidas*'s being, in intention or in achievement, a poem 'nearly anonymous'. It may be useful, then, to examine an opposite view of the poem: at Mr. Robert Graves's view of *Lycidas* as a poem 'strangled with art'.

II

What worries Mr. Graves, as it worried Dr. Johnson, is that the very care and pains which Milton took to make *Lycidas* the most perfect verbal art-work, perhaps, of its length in the English language do seem also to make it clear that Milton had no strong personal feelings of grief about Edward King. Personal grief, if it expresses itself at all in poetry, does not express itself in this way; Bossuet's great *oraisons funèbres* are art-works in a sense comparable to *Lycidas*, but one does not suspect that Bossuet cared twopence for Madame or for the Prince. He uses these great personages as pegs for tremendous meditations on the transitoriness of all earthly glory, and yet allows that it *is* glorious; he uses worldliness to reinforce unction. This was a typically seventeenth-century thing to do, and though Bossuet outrageously flattered his great dead personages, and skirted over those scandalous aspects of their lives with which his auditory was perfectly familiar, the emotion of these great orations was perfectly sincere.

It is an emotion of that baroque kind, though deeper and purer, that we must look for in *Lycidas*. For Bossuet, Madame ceases to be a person, becomes simply the Great Lady; the Prince ceases to be a person, becomes simply the Hero. And similarly Milton in *Lycidas* is not lamenting King as a person; he is lamenting the Young Poet; and the young poet is, because of the very roots of the tradition of the pastoral elegy, the Dying God, and the Dying God is a forerunner of Christ, who alone of all the Dying Gods has conquered Death, and given us an assurance that we may conquer it. Yet, for all that assurance, the fact that we do die remains an outrage on the unity of Nature. It is important, for instance, that Orpheus comes in at a key point of the poem. Orpheus is the type of all poets. But he is also a kind of prefiguration of Christ. Like Christ he descends into Hell and comes out again; but, where Christ harrows Hell, Orpheus loses Eurydice at the last moment. Like Christ as the Logos, Orpheus harmonizes the natural world with his music. Like Christ, he is cruelly sacrificed, but, unlike Christ, he has no resurrection. The Muse who bore him cannot bring him to life again, and the Muse is not only 'golden-haired Calliope', she is 'Universal nature'. Nature, or the feminine principle, gives life but cannot conquer death. If we wish to inherit eternal life, we must rely on something above Nature, on the 'dear might of him that walked the waves'. This fusion—not confusion, as Johnson thought—of pagan and Christian ideas is the central strength of the poem. *Lycidas,* as Professor R. L. Brett has recently pointed out, was the last poem in which Milton was able to fuse Christian and pagan imagery in this way and to see nature as, in a sense, sacramental. A sacramental view of nature went naturally with the baroque style and with the Counter-Reformation, but Milton's Puritanism tugged the other way. He was a Platonist as well as a Puritan, and while one aspect of the Platonic, or neo-Platonic, tradition could see nature as a set of imperfect symbols of a divine or ideal real world, another aspect of it exalted reason (as Puritanism exalted faith, or the indwelling spirit) at the expense of the senses. Milton was moving steadily towards a greater austerity, in *Paradise Lost* the images and figures of pagan mythology have become either demons or distorted echoes of the truth about the Garden of Eden: *Paradise Regained* and *Samson Agonistes* are in a very bare, austere style, without even the ornament. Professor Brett suggests that

> Tomorrow to fresh Woods and Pastures new,

is a farewell to the whole pastoral mode with its ambiguous mythologies. And Professor Frank Kermode has pointed out to me that Milton, while writing *Lycidas,* was pretty near the end of the *sapientia veterum* tradition in imagery, the tradition which saw in pagan mythology a prefiguration of Christian truth, which saw in it even a kind of obscure revelation to the Gentiles. In a note to me, Professor Kermode writes: 'It is a large question whether the decay of the *veterum sapientia* tradition had to do with the retrenchment of the Christian empire; perhaps it was only that better (different) history made it inconceivable that the pagan emblems should be fundamentally Christian. There was, anyway, only a temporary lull in this attitude; since we all know today that Orpheus does "mean" Christ, and so forth.'

In his remarks about the 'retrenchment of the Christian Empire', Professor Kermode was referring to something I had said in an earlier draft of this essay: I had said that one could excuse Dr. Johnson for not liking *Lycidas*, for hating the fusion of pagan and Christian ideas, because he was writing in another age, when Christian belief could no longer expand, like a great conqueror, over the whole universe of pagan symbols, but had to contract, like a declining Empire, and sullenly protect itself. I added rather rashly that no two adjacent centuries had ever been more startlingly unlike each other, in the very fibre of their minds, than the seventeenth and eighteenth. That generalization was too rash; Milton was a classic, perhaps the only real English classic (Shakespeare being great but untidy) for eighteenth-century writers; and it is clear from what Professor Brett says that the kind of contraction of Christian sympathy away from pagan images, the defensive attitude, which I had ascribed to Dr. Johnson, was in fact becoming partly Milton's own attitude, even as he was writing *Lycidas* itself. Between the Christian and the pagan images in the poem Professor Brett finds not confusion like Johnson, or mainly rich fusion like Miss Tuve, but centrally a dramatic irresolvable tension.

I have got rather far from Mr. Graves. With his classical learning, Mr. Graves ought to have seen most or all of what I have been expounding, but his strong personal antipathy to Milton makes him naughty. He says sharply:

> There is authentic emotion in *Lycidas*, but it springs, as in [Milton's] *Lament for Damon*, from the realization that young intellectuals of [Milton's] generation are as liable as anyone else to die suddenly; Fate's latest victim might well have been John Milton, not Edward King; which would have been a far more serious literary disaster.

This is to take the poem very pettily, and to ignore the tradition to which *Lycidas* belongs. It is clear that at the time of the Renaissance Christian belief gave a new depth to the revived pastoral elegy. Yet this highly artificial and sophisticated form had possessed a certain depth from the first. The depth came partly from the mysteries; it came partly from the new self-consciousness (something unclassical) of the early Hellenistic world, from the discovery in Alexandrian libraries of man's inner self, which would never have been discovered in the Agora. It sprang from the indignant refusal to accept death, from the plaintive hope of some kind of ultimate resurrection. In Theocritus' elegy for Daphnis, the nymphs are reproached, as they are reproached in Milton, for not protecting the young man:

> Where were ye, Nymphs, oh where, while Daphnis pined?
> In fair Peneus or in Pindus' glen,

and 'Universal nature' also, in parcels, laments:

> O'er him the wolves, the jackals howled o'er him;
> The lion in the oak-copse mourned his death. . . .

And in Bion's lament for Adonis, resurrection may never happen, but the mourning must go on, year after year:

> *Woe!* and *Ah for Adonis!* the Muses who wail for Adonis,
> Chaunt their charms to Adonis.—But he lists not to their singing;
> Not that he wills not to hear, but the Maiden doth not release him.
> Cease from moans, Cytherea, today refrain from the death-songs;
> Thou must lament him again, and again shed tears in a new year.

And for Moschus, Bion has himself become Orpheus:

> The Dorian Orpheus, tell them all, is dead,

and in the underworld he may perhaps charm Persephone into letting him go:

> Nor will thy singing unrewarded be;
> Thee to the mountain-haunts she will restore,
> As she gave Orpheus his Eurydice.
> Could I charm Dis with songs, I too would sing for thee.

Milton's great poem is in a sense the crown of this whole tradition not because he feels the general outrage of death any more deeply than Theocritus or Bion or Moschus, but because he has a firmer hope to build on: Edward King is in Heaven at the end of Milton's poem not as a pleasing fancy, as a dallying with false surmise, but firmly as fact. The dear might of Him who walked the waves is something far more firmly to be relied on than the possible good nature of Persephone or than the yearly death and birth of Adonis, which is merely the death of winter and the birth of spring, the bursting of the seed and the sprouting of the young corn. It does not matter much, I think, whether we as modern readers cling to the Christian hope or not; Milton's own clinging is firm enough to make the poem work for us, and the fact that, as modern readers, we accept his Orpheus so easily makes it simpler for us to accept, also, his Christ. We can take it all as mythology, if we like, but as mythology very powerfully organized; and it does release in us as in Milton very powerful emotions.

Mr. Graves refuses to see all this because he has his own kind of theological odium; he does not really want God set above the Muse, and perhaps he feels that a happy ending to this sort of story is vulgar; it is better that Adonis should be dead for good, and that Cytherea should weep for ever. But for Mr. Graves, also, Milton is a kind of archetypal anti-poet, because a true poet writes for love, not for the love of art, and Milton, he thinks, with all the gifts of a genuine minor poet and with a quite exceptional ear for music, was incapable of love, and allowed diabolical ambition to swell him up into big poet. Mr. Graves does, in fact, admit that the music of *Lycidas* is very powerful; so powerful, he thinks, that it distracts Milton from attending to the sense of what he is saying.

The music, of course, is Italianate; as Professor F. T. Prince has shown, Milton learned much from the *canzoni* of sixteenth-century Italian poets like Tasso, particularly in his use of 'hanging' or unrhymed lines and of lines of uneven length. He learned something also from Italian pastoral drama. Mr. Graves thinks that Milton may also have learned something from Welsh poetic tradition, particularly his cunning use of 'consonantal chime', subtly interwoven. I italicize in this passage the consonants, voiced dentals, liquids, aspirates, semi-vowels, to which Mr. Graves calls particular attention:

> For Lycidas is *d*ea*d*, *d*ea*d* ere his prime,
> Young Lycidas, and *h*ath not *l*eft his *p*eer:
> *Wh*o would not sing for Lycidas? he *kn*ew

*H*imself to sing, and bui*ld* the *l*ofty rime.
He must not f*l*oat upon his *wa*try bear
Un*w*ept, and *w*elter to the parching *w*ind,
*W*ithout the meed of som me*lod*ious tear.

I have not italicized the more crude and obvious alliterations of labials there ('build', 'bear', or 'meed . . . melodious'). They perhaps serve mainly to distract the reader's attention from the more cunning concealed consonantal patterning. Mr. Graves comments:

> The exigencies of his complicated metrical scheme have blurred the logic of the stanza—*parching* and *melodious* are . . . examples of words chosen for their sound at the expense of meaning—but his musical craftsmanship has lulled successive generations of readers into delighted acquiescence, and in Johnson's words 'driven away the eye from nice examination'.

How far are these two particular strictures just? The tear, of course, is a metaphor for an elegy, and though a tear cannot be melodious an elegy can, and *Lycidas* conspicuously is: 'melodious' is literal and 'tear' is metaphorical. I do not know whether there is a name for this rhetorical device, but one can think of other examples of it like Cleveland's 'keen iambics' (they are literally iambics but only metaphorically keen or cutting) or Milton's own 'Jonson's learned sock' (Jonson's comedies were literally learned, but only by synecdoche socks; because Roman actors wore socks in comedy, buskins, or high-heeled shoes, in tragedy). The epithet 'parching', however, is certainly harder to justify. Floating, drowned and bloated on the top of the sea, Lycidas ought not, even if we attribute to his dead body some kind of consciousness, to bother much about whether it is raining or not. He is wet enough already: 'Too much of water hast thou, poor Ophelia!' Soaked as he is, he might in fact want to be dried: but 'parching' has connotations of active and painful deprivation. Let us see if we can find some way to circumvent what seems, at first sight, Mr. Graves's very cogent objection.

I think we can justify 'parching', in a very round-about way, in the total context of the poem. It is now almost a commonplace (I forget who first worked the idea out) that *Lycidas* is a poem strangely full of water-images, sometimes suggesting destruction, but often refreshment or purification. One of these images is that of the poet inspired by *drinking* at a sacred fountain or stream:

> O Fountain *Arethuse*, and thou honourd flood,
> Smooth-sliding *Mincius*, crownd with vocal reeds. . . .

Drowning is not drinking, but the very opposite: we may fancy that raindrops out of the sky, fresh water, could give the floating, drowned, but still in some sense conscious Lycidas rest or refreshment, cleanse or soothe him. He floats, after all, in salt or brackish water. The phrase 'fountain, shade, and rill' has come earlier in the poem; Deva's 'wizard stream' comes in later; the sea itself is magicked to benignity:

> The Air was calm, and on the level brine
> Sleek *Panope* with all her sisters playd,

and the happy ending of the poem is when Lycidas quenches his thirst and cleanses his limbs in Heaven: through the strength of Christ who conquered the treachery of water;

> So *Lycidas* sunk low, but mounted high
> Through the dear might of him that walkd the waves;
> Where other groves and other streams along,
> With *Nectar* pure his oozy Locks he laves,
> And hears the unexpressive nuptial Song.

('Unexpressive' there—it is the penalty of writing in an unsettled language—means the opposite of what we mean by 'unexpressive': it means too beautiful for Milton to attempt to convey an impression of it—inexpressible.) The streams, there, stand again for refreshment, and it is with a life-giving liquor, with nectar, that Lycidas washes the death-giving liquid, or earth-water compound, ooze, out of his hair. Water brings both death and life. At the back of Milton's mind were concepts like hungering and *thirsting* after righteousness; like drinking the communion cup (Anglicans in Milton's time were offered the cup as well as the bread, where Continental Papists had to be content with the wafer). The 'nectar pure' might also have some connection with the oil of extreme unction—though this is something that Milton would have with his conscious mind disapproved of—and certainly with the water of baptism. Taking all these points together,

I feel that the epithet 'parching' can be justified against Mr. Graves.

When we are told in fact (as not only Mr. Graves but Dr. Leavis tells us, and as Mr. Eliot tells us in his earlier criticisms of Milton) that Milton has a weakness for subordinating possible subtlety of sense to an easily attainable effectiveness of sound, we should remember one of the earliest memorable judgements on Milton's language, that of the early eighteenth-century painter and critic, Jonathan Richardson:

> A Reader of *Milton* must be always upon Duty; he is surrounded with Sense, it rises in every Line, every Word is to the Purpose; There are no Lazy Intervals, All has been Consider'd, and Demands, and Merits Observation. Even in the Best Writers you Sometimes find Words and Sentences which hang on so Loosely you may Blow 'em Off; *Milton's* are all Substance and Weight; Fewer would not have Serv'd the Turn, and More would have been Superfluous.

Mr. Eliot's early judgement on Milton has in fact something in common with Mr. Graves's. I quote a famous passage, bringing in *Lycidas*, from Mr. Eliot's 'A Note on the Verse of John Milton' (1936):

> . . . I suspect also that this concentration upon the auditory imagination leads to at least an occasional levity. I can enjoy the roll of
>
> . . . Cambula, seat of Cathaian Can
> And Samarkand by Oxus, Temir's throne,
> To Paquin of Sinaean kings, and thence
> To Agra and Lahor of great Mogul
> Down to the golden Chersonese, or where
> The Persian in Ecbatan sate, or since
> In Hispahan, or where the Russian Ksar
> In Mosco, or the Sultan in Bizance,
> Turchestan-born . . .
>
> and the rest of it, but I feel that this is not serious poetry, not poetry fully occupied about its business, but rather a solemn game. More often, admittedly, Milton uses proper names in moderation, to obtain the same effect of magnificence with them

as does Marlowe—nowhere perhaps better than in the passage from *Lycidas*:

> Whether beyond the stormy Hebrides,
> Where thou perhaps under the whelming tide
> Visit'st the bottom of the monstrous world;
> Or whether thou to our moist vows deny'd
> Sleep'st by the fable of Bellerus old,
> Where the great vision of the guarded Mount
> Looks toward Namancos and Bayona's hold. . . .

than which, for the single effect of grandeur in sound, there is nothing finer in poetry. . . .

The tribute is grudging in one sense, but generous in another, and it may be in fact that when most of us first come across the 'stormy Hebrides' passage the 'grandeur of sound' is enough for us. But we are still, in Richardson's phrase, 'surrounded by sense', which 'rises in every line'. Washed by the tides along the west coast of our island, King's body might be carried north to the Hebrides or south to St. Michael's Mount in Cornwall. Near the Hebrides he may be 'visiting' (Miss Tuve has pointed out the fine irony of the word) the bottom of the sea, 'monstrous' because it is full of monsters who are terrifying, parodic or distorted-mirror. 'Our moist vows' has the same kind of irony as 'visit'st': poor King has moisture enough. The fable of the Cornish giant Bellerus fits in, for tone, with the monsters at the bottom of the sea. But St. Michael, on his mount, which has in fact a ruined castle on top of it, and which is also still guarded by him, looks across the unbroken stretch of sea towards Namancos—towards Spain and the Inquisition from which he is guarding England—and towards the castle at Bayona which is the counterpart to the ruin on his mount. The sense has a richness which matches the richness of the sound.

The kind of richness of sense which *Lycidas* possesses is not, however, the same kind of richness that we admire, say, in Donne or in Pope. It is not a richness in which, so to say, all the strands of meaning have their ends neatly tied together, and about which we can say, having completed an exhaustive analysis, 'This, this, and this, the poem means, and no more.' The meaning, rather, lies in layers of growing extension combined with growing depth.

Miss Tuve makes this point against Dr. Johnson. He had said in a famous passage:

> In this poem there is no nature, for there is nothing new. Its form is that of a pastoral, easy, vulgar, and therefore disgusting; whatever images it can supply are long ago exhausted, and its inherent improbability always forces dissatisfaction of the mind. When Cowley tells of Hervey, that they studied together, it is easy to suppose how much he must miss the companion of his labours, and the partner of his discoveries; but what image of tenderness can be excited by these lines?—
>
> We drove a field, and both together heard
> What time the grey fly winds her sultry horn,
> Battening our flocks with the fresh dews of night.
>
> We know that they never drove a field, and that they had no flocks to batten; and though it be allowed that the representation may be allegorical, the true meaning is so uncertain and remote that it is never sought because it cannot be known when it is found.

Where Dr. Johnson has gone wrong there, Miss Tuve seems to feel, is in seeking for the meaning of allegory, or indeed of metaphor, in a kind of point-to-point correspondence; as if, for instance, the field in which the young scholars drove might be their libraries, their flocks their books, as if the fresh dews of night stood for late reading that did not lead to staleness, and as if the grey fly winding her sultry horn stood perhaps for their more frivolous fellow students, their chatter adding to the pleasantness of the university atmosphere, but not really distracting Milton and King from their studies. It would certainly be mad to read, or attempt to read, the poem that way. But one should quote Miss Tuve:

> Dr. Johnson, in the passage on *Lycidas* which made 'no flocks to batten' so famous, clearly thinks of allegory as a set of synonymous correspondences, and when he says 'the true meaning is so uncertain and remote that . . . it cannot be known when it is found', he marks as a vice what provides the strength of allegory as it does of metaphor; that which speaks of things in their universal consideration must of necessity present meanings not certainly limited.

Dr. Johnson, she feels, had not sympathetically lived through the history of pastoral metaphors. We are able today to feel a sympathy for Milton's way of using allegory and metaphor which was out of the reach of a purely or narrowly Augustan critic like Dr. Johnson (one might note that he was as much out of sympathy with Gray's *Odes*, experiments in the Miltonic or 'sublime' lyrical mode, as he was out of sympathy with *Lycidas*). If we explore the history of pastoral metaphor and allegory, of the pastoral mode, 'we may see again one of the faces of truth which was turned aside from the eighteenth century'.

We may, as it were, cease to seek to pin-point meanings in poetry, but be ready instead, as when a pebble is dropped in a pool, to watch meanings opening out in rings. One of the great cruces in *Lycidas*, for instance, is the passage at the end of St. Peter's speech:

> 'But that two-handed engin at the door,
> 'Stands ready to smite once, and smite no more.'

Bridges thought that this passage was prophetic; the 'two-handed engin' is a headsman's axe, and Milton was foreseeing the execution of Charles I. A more sane and sober explanation is that it is the two Houses of Parliament standing on guard outside the sheepfold (or outside the Church of England) and ready, by punitive legislation, to smite 'the grim Wolf with privy paw', or the Romish intruder, once and for all. There are, Miss Tuve tells us, about eight-and-twenty explanations on the market. For her, the most deeply and widely valid one is a reference to the Day of Judgement, to the final reckoning which all sinners must face. Miss Tuve is nothing if not an enthusiast; and I hope one is not showing a Johnsonian over-literalness, and blindness to 'one of the faces of truth', in wondering whether 'the sword that issues from the mouth of God' in the book of Revelations is, in fact, strictly speaking a 'two-handed instrument'—hands are not involved in its wielding—and what 'door' it strictly stands at, or waits at. My instinct is that, however deeply or widely one can profitably take him, Milton at least *meant* a topical and political allusion here; and I do not think that he was by temperament the sort of man who would wait patiently for the Day of Judgement for his enemies to get their deserts.

Miss Tuve's 'Theme, Pattern and Imagery in *Lycidas*', in her book *Images and Themes in Five Poems by Milton* is the finest essay I know on the poem, and the essay which, I think conclusively, answers Mr. Graves's accusation that Milton was an unloving man and that *Lycidas* is a poem 'strangled by art'. It is to be noted, however, that she does not seek to find in the poem the personal tenderness which Johnson found lacking in it, or, indeed, the special kind of human interest which he always looked for first and foremost in a poem. She is not saying that it is a good poem by Augustan standards, but that Augustan standards are too narrow. The kind of love she finds in it is neither a personal love for King nor Milton's self-love; the kind of tenderness she finds is cosmic, rather than human in the Augustan sense. The final claim she makes for the poem, and for the pastoral mode of which it is perhaps the crowning achievement, is this:

> Pastoral has its ways of reasserting a fundamental and harmonious sympathy, and of proclaiming that not decay and death but life and creativity and love is the universal principle, one which is seen (especially, but not solely, as pastoral was Christianized) as having the strength of a divine intention.

She notes, also, very usefully, that one great difficulty in the way of our responding, today, to a poem like *Lycidas*, is our sense of separateness from nature and the separative ways in which we have learned to use language and, therefore, to think. Universal Nature could not lament in a modern poem nor could the wolves and jackals howl over Daphnis. I quote Miss Tuve again on this:

> The harmony among the creatures is by no means necessarily pagan even when its terms are so; the point around which the matter turns is rather whether the metaphors which express it are believed or not. Figures which adumbrate it use the so-called pathetic fallacy as their natural language, but they mean what they say. Such language neither denies a hierarchy among creatures nor a special tie between man and divinity; its giving man's form of sentience or will or *pathos* to other creatures is a metaphorical way of putting unity not identity.

And in a footnote she adds further clarifications:

> Nor is the unity in a sympathetic harmony contradicted by the famous figure of the 'riddle' of man's short earthly life (his

never coming again contrasted with the cyclical renewal of other creatures); Man is no more seen as outside 'Nature' because he does not sprout again like the tree than the tree is fallaciously made 'Man' when the metaphor of human responses (it sighs, it mourns) is used. The conceptions really antipathetic to these ways of thinking and using language are nominalistic conceptions of metaphor, or naturalistic or positivistic conceptions of what meanings can be real. Milton did not share them.

III

To have nominalistic conceptions of metaphor can, I think, be shown to be an intellectual error; it can be shown that it is not by point-to-point correspondence to particularistic 'tenors' that metaphor, as a 'vehicle', works; though it would be possible to construct such nominalistic metaphors, and in the more trivial kinds of metaphysical or cavalier light verse one sometimes finds them (Suckling, for instance, has an indecent little poem about a candle, in which the candle is a point-to-point metaphor for the penis). On the other hand, though 'Milton did not share them', I suppose many modern lovers of poetry have 'naturalistic or positivistic conceptions of what meanings can be real', not out of a wrong-headed perversity, but because, after thought and inquiry, they have decided that such conceptions are true. What, apart from its sheer beauty—which is much, and which for some readers might perhaps be everything—has a poem like *Lycidas* to offer to such readers? Such readers can arrive, if they make the effort, at the kind of deep and wide meaning which Miss Tuve finds in *Lycidas*, but they may find it a meaning possible to conceive, possible to sympathize with, possible to accept 'poetically', but not, in the end, possible to accept as 'real'. They may feel simply that we have no moral or intellectual *right* to believe that 'not decay and death but life and creativity is the universal principle', that there is a great deal of evidence in the sad history of the world suggesting that this is not so, and that, even if it is not so, we have the duty of building up, within our own lives, what life and creativity we can: knowing, or fearing, that such life and creativity is perishable.

I imagine that I am describing a fairly widespread contemporary state of mind. People in this state of mind have a sympathy with

Dr. Johnson; they may feel that a 'cosmic' poem like *Lycidas*, wonderful and rich and deep and consoling as it is, in the end begs too many questions; and that a 'human' poem like Johnson's own elegy on Dr. Levett, bare and down to earth as it is in comparison, is more concerned with matters of human experience that lend themselves to testing.

And to other poets, like Mr. Graves, the 'cosmic' tenderness of *Lycidas* will seem less valuable, for all Milton's elaborate and consummate art, than the tenderness of humbler poems springing directly out of personal relationships. An essay like this cannot, I think, and ought not to, aim at altering anybody's bias of this sort. But a few very general reflections on this problem of poetry and belief, or perhaps of poetry and the general direction of one's interests, as that affects *Lycidas*, may be helpful.

There are a number of possible ways out of this wood. One is simply this: the creation, the existence, the survival, the impact upon ourselves of a poem like *Lycidas* is, surely, a very important part of the evidence we have that 'not decay and death but life and creativity is the universal principle'. Just as great poetical works that seem to express something near utter despair, like Shakespeare's *Troilus and Cressida*, for instance, contradict their message by the magnificence with which they manage to state their message—and if merely that was true in the end, why take all that trouble to say it?—so, contrariwise, great poems which, looking at the worst, emerge with the grand assertion that all, nevertheless, is somehow well, seem to guarantee by their impact the relevance of their impact. What positivist or naturalist, what linguistic analyst, faced, say, with the last stanza of Yeats's 'Among School Children'—allow the man some modicum of sensibility—would burst out with, 'Oh, but it's not true!'? Art *makes* truth, its own kind of truth.

And poetry is, more perhaps than Miss Tuve allows, a special sort of language. When I mentioned to William Empson the gap between ourselves and Milton in *Lycidas*, of which she speaks in her essay, because we feel separate from universal Nature, and he did not, Empson, in his usual, blunt sensible way, pointed out for practical purposes, in everyday life, Milton felt just as separate as we do. He could write with absolute conviction, in poetry:

And, O ye dolphins, waft the hapless youth.

He would not, foundering at sea, have looked, any more than King did, for a dolphin. And on the other hand, healthy men in our own time may as much as Milton feel a kind of unity with nature, though they have no concepts to justify it, and no images by which they can convey the feeling very convincingly in poetry. But we all know, for instance, the feeling of inner death and the slow process of inner rebirth; and to this feeling *Lycidas* in its way can speak as convincingly as *The Ancient Mariner* or *The Waste Land.* Perhaps we are more at home in the cosmos, and in cosmic imagery, than we think. We know in our hearts that great art, or great joy, or great love, cannot be made out of an *enclosedly* human world, a world that shuts out intimations that naturalism and positivism cannot justify. And I would like to close these random reflections by another quotation from Miss Tuve, to whose packed insights I owe so much:

> The universal use of figurative terms from the pastoral life for these literal historical meanings makes *our history itself present* to us much profounder significances of storm and wild ravager, and we read constantly in pastoral of two worlds, both that of our particular human disasters and that which can organize only through our symbols of a Waste Land, of Garden given over to thorns, Harmony become chaos—and, of the Garden of Adonis, the Earthly Paradise, and the perfect music of the spheres.

I admire Milton enormously but I find it hard to like him much (Empson remarked to me, in this same conversation, that though all poets are vain or conceited, Milton was the only one who wanted God to pat him on the head for writing such good verses). There is something true in what De Quincey says, and it explains how impossible it is not to admire him, how difficult to like him: 'Repulsion was the law of his being; he moved in solitary grandeur.' He moves in less solitary grandeur, I think, in *Lycidas* than anywhere else. No poem, of that length, in the English language, is more through and through an art-work; yet what other poem of that length touches so vividly, or so deeply, the primal sympathies?

IV

THE OPENING OF *PARADISE LOST*

David Daiches

EVERY SCHOOLBOY knows that in the opening twenty-six lines of *Paradise Lost* Milton is following the tradition of classical epic in announcing his subject and invoking the Muse, and that at the same time he asserts that his subject is greater than that of classical epic and his Muse no classical Muse but the very Spirit of God. A close look at this obviously carefully meditated opening passage reveals not only the remarkable cunning with which Milton managed its structure and its cadence but also many of the characteristic ways in which he handled language, the kinds of use he made of echoes of background reference, the different degrees of weight he gave to words, his techniques of emphasis, his deliberate counterpointing of abstract and concrete, his awareness of himself as poet facing a given audience, and many other aspects of his art. Though there is a full-stop at the end of the sixteenth line, the whole passage constitutes a single (but not a simple) movement in its intellectual and emotional pattern as well as in its appeal to the ear:

> Of Mans First Disobedience, and the Fruit
> Of that Forbidden Tree, whose mortal tast
> Brought Death into the World, and all our woe,
> With loss of *Eden*, till one greater Man
> Restore us, and regain the blissful Seat,
> Sing Heav'nly Muse, that on the secret top

Of *Oreb*, or of *Sinai*, didst inspire
That Shepherd, who first taught the chosen Seed,
In the Beginning how the Heav'ns and Earth
Rose out of *Chaos*: Or if *Sion* Hill
Delight thee more, and *Siloa's* Brook that flowd
Fast by the Oracle of God; I thence
Invoke thy aid to my adventrous Song,
That with no middle flight intends to soar
Above th' *Aonian* Mount; while it persues
Things unattempted yet in Prose or Rime.
And chiefly Thou O Spirit, that dost preferr
Before all Temples th' upright heart and pure,
Instruct me, for Thou knowst; Thou from the first
Wast present, and with mighty wing outspread
Dove-like satst brooding on the vast Abyss
And mad'st it pregnant: What in mee is dark
Illumin, what is low raise and support;
That to the highth of this great Argument
I may assert Eternal Providence,
And justifie the wayes of God to men.

The opening phrase, 'Of Mans First Disobedience', has extraordinary weight and emphasis; it is also austere in its simplicity and bears the rhythm of its own gravity rather than of an imposed metre. Emphasis falls on the second and third words and on the first and third syllables of 'Disobedience' (for I should contend that Milton is emphasizing that it is *dis*obedience and is not simply skipping over the first syllable to say 'disobédience'). The beat is: 'Of MANS FIRST DISoBEdience,' with the emphasis on the first syllable of 'disobedience' slowing down the rhythm and effectively preventing any mechanical iambic pentameter run. Indeed, the three emphatic syllables together give an effect of deliberateness, of carefully weighed enunciation, that compels attention. Yet we are not allowed to pause; the sense moves on at once with 'and the Fruit / Of that Forbidden Tree, . . .' The ear is immediately struck by the alliteration 'First . . . Fruit . . . Forbidden.' The alliteration forces these words together: we think of 'first fruit', then—'forbidden'. The twenty-third chapter of Leviticus gives the divine command to the children of Israel concerning the festival of the firstfruits. 'When ye be come unto the land which I give unto you, and shall reap the harvest thereof, then ye shall bring a sheaf of the firstfruits of your harvest unto the priest: And he shall wave the sheaf before the Lord, to be accepted for you: . . .' An audience deeply familiar with the Old Testament could scarcely help hearing an echo of this passage behind the opening two lines of *Paradise Lost.* The echo is achieved by alliteration. 'First Fruit Forbidden'—not brought before the Lord to be accepted, but forbidden. The *perversity* of the situation is apparent. Man's first disobedience was for Milton the primal perversity, and he manages to suggest this in his opening by using what might be called purely acoustical means of achieving a biblical echo—an echo which is also a distortion.

This primal perversity is man's: 'Mans First Disobedience'. Milton must be using the large collective term 'Man' advisedly: at the end of the passage he uses the phrase 'justifie the wayes of God to men'—not 'to man', though it is often thus mis-quoted. Adam represented his kind, and his act was representative, man's act. Milton's audience, on the other hand, was a particular community in a particular time and place, men to man. We remember the soul-searching undergone by Milton before he decided to limit his audience by writing in his native language rather than in Latin. For all the sublime self-confidence of this opening, with Milton seeing himself as playing the role of Moses, inspired by the Holy Spirit, he does not claim to speak to the world but only to some people in it. A seventeenth-century Puritan was only too conscious of the difference between the sheep and the goats, and certainly Milton by the time he came to write *Paradise Lost* was very much aware of himself as a member of a small elect to whom alone he could talk. One might thus connect his use of the word 'men' in the phrase 'justifie the wayes of God to men' with that passage at the beginning of Book VII where he asks Urania to 'fit audience find, though few'.

In the second line Milton allows the iambic pentameter rhythm to establish itself. It would not do to persevere too long after the opening in a rhythm determined purely by the demands of the intellectual and rhetorical pattern; the regular beat of the blank verse must make itself heard while there is still time to establish it as the underlying beat of the poem. So the line 'Of that Forbidden Tree, whose mortal tast' sounds this beat clearly and enables us—

retroactively, as it were—to hear the first line as a metrical deviation forced on the poet by the gravity and intensity of his opening words. This is not to argue that the best way of listening to Milton's verse is to think of a line made up of five iambic feet as the norm from which every now and again he deliberately deviates in order to achieve certain effects. Milton did not compose in terms of separable feet but in terms of the rhythmic phrase. But he did of course have a basic rhythmic movement with respect to which variations could be seen as variations having particular effects. I do not propose, however, in this discussion to go into this aspect of Milton's art.[1]

In spite of the deliberate leaning on the words 'Mans First Disobedience' there is no lingering on vowels in the first two lines of the poem; the vowels are for the most part rather clipped and enclosed by consonants. This makes the last three words of the third line—'all our woe'—with their three contiguous long vowels singing out dolefully one after the other all the more effective. Vowel sounds in themselves, of course, can suggest anything or nothing; but in this context, and in association with words of this particular meaning, the vowels and diphthongs of 'all our woe' sound like a veritable wail of grief. The whole line slows down and language itself seems to dissolve into inarticulate keening, 'aaw—aoo—oh'. But the dissolution is momentary; we are recalled at once to what the words *say*: '*all* our woe', the sheer abundance of it, all human woe is attributable to this primal sin; 'all *our* woe'—not only Adam's and Eve's but ours too, for the consequences of the eating of the forbidden fruit are still with us; 'all our *woe*'—the penalty of Adam's sin was and is woe. The wailful phrase sums up centuries of theological commentary on the Fall. And it is the meaning that controls the sound and determines that each of the three words gets equal emphasis.

The almost parenthetical 'with loss of Eden' which follows at the beginning of the fourth line seems at first sight to be a good phrase thrown away, as though loss of Eden was a little extra woe thrown in. But Milton is surely playing it down deliberately. Later in the poem he makes very clear what loss of Eden involves. Here he touches for a bare moment on this stupendous theme, and the refusal to elaborate provides (or so it seems to me) a note of

[1] See F. T. Prince, *The Italian Element in Milton's Verse* (Oxford, 1954).

suspense and foreboding: the very casualness is sinister. It is also significant that Eden is mentioned for the first time in the poem in connection with the word 'loss': later on we see Eden for the first time—through Satan's eyes. As for the continuation, 'till one greater Man / Restore us, and regain the blissful Seat', this has the air of recapitulating a known lesson. It sounds hurried and even deliberately perfunctory, and even if we see a suspicion of Milton's Arianism in his description of Jesus as 'one greater Man' it is clear that in terms of the movement of this whole passage the phrase bears no great weight. The real burden of the poem is not *here*. Posterity has seen fit to sneer at Thomas Ellwood's remark to Milton on reading *Paradise Lost* that 'Thou hast said much here of Paradise Lost, but what hast thou to say of Paradise Found?' on the grounds that Milton told the whole story, of Paradise Lost *and* Found, in *Paradise Lost*. But Ellwood was perfectly right in his implication; 'till one greater Man / Restore us, and regain the blissful Seat' is only perfunctorily a part of *Paradise Lost*, a poem into which the Christian scheme of redemption is not emotionally integrated at all. And here in the introductory statement of theme it is recited almost mechanically like a school lesson. Milton does not even bother to make clear what he means by 'regain the blissful Seat'. Does the 'greater Man' regain the blissful Seat for himself or for the first man or for all men? In any case, I would maintain that there is a deliberately routine quality about the second half of line 4 and line 5, and this links up with the fact that *Paradise Lost* is not about the 'fortunate fall' in the sense that it tells how man's fall brought forth the Christian scheme of redemption (the account of which occupies a very small and unemphatic part of the poem) but about the fall as exhibiting the paradox of man's nature and his destiny. Further, the phrase 'the blissful Seat' is deliberately abstract and in its context almost meaningless—certainly it has much less meaning than the simple word 'Eden' dropped so lightly yet significantly in line 4. How much more meaning Milton gets into the phrase 'so late thir happie seat' at the end of the poem, when the whole weight of the completed epic lies behind the words.

This is not to argue that the second half of line 4 and line 5 are bad, but rather to assert that the force of the preceding phrase 'all our woe' is such that it controls the meaning of the turn towards restoration and bliss, deliberately keeping it formal and deprived of full emotional realization, so that Milton seems to be saying: 'Though I will include a reference to the Christian scheme of redemption in my epic, the full realized meaning of the poem concerns the nature of the Fall and its consequences and not the redemption.' And that indeed is the truth about *Paradise Lost*.

The first five lines state the theme, as the object of 'Sing Heav'nly Muse', a phrase which rings out with serene confidence at the beginning of line 6. The inversion of subject and object here is no mere piece of barren classicism, but a device for keeping fluidity of movement in the whole opening section. 'Of Mans First Disobedience . . . Sing Heav'nly Muse, that on the secret top / Of *Oreb*, or of *Sinai*, didst inspire / That Shepherd, who first taught . . .' The concatenation of phrases here, with 'the sense variously drawn out from one Verse into another', is most artfully managed. We are swept forward, without being allowed to pause, until Milton has identified his Muse and placed himself with relation to the Muse and to his audience. The relative pronouns ('that on the secret top . . .,' 'who first taught the chosen Seed') prevent us from pausing, keep us moving along. The 'Heav'nly Muse' is defined as soon as invoked—defined as God Himself who, in secret communion with Moses on Mount Horeb (Milton here uses the Vulgate form without the 'h', something he does fairly often with Old Testament names presumably for reasons of euphony), first revealed himself to him. 'Now Moses kept the flock of Jethro his father-in-law, the priest of Midian: and he led the flock to the back side of the desert, and came to the mountain of God, even to Horeb. And the Angel of the Lord appeared unto him in a flame of fire out of the midst of a bush: and he looked, and, behold, the bush burned with fire, and the bush was not consumed. And Moses said, I will now turn aside, and see this great sight, why the bush is not burnt. And when the Lord saw that he turned aside to see, God called unto him out of the midst of the bush, and said, Moses, Moses. And he said, Here am I.' It was as a shepherd that Moses went to Horeb, a fact which Milton emphasizes with a curiously casual nod in the direction of the biblical story—'*That* Shepherd.' There is here a quiet confidence that his readers know all about the biblical story; the word 'that' establishes Milton's common knowledge with his audience, almost as though he is saying, 'that shepherd whom we know all about'. It is also important that he first refers to Moses as a shepherd, a word full of overtones both in pastoral and in religious tradition. On Horeb Moses was still just a shepherd; on Mount Sinai he was a leader of men and a prophet of God. 'The secret top / Of *Oreb*, or of *Sinai*' brings together these two aspects of Moses and associates them both with his own status as poet, so that both Moses and Milton become the shepherd-prophet-poet, which is precisely the function of the ideal shepherd in *Lycidas*. It was on Sinai that Moses is first fully revealed as the inspired spokesman of God. 'And Moses went up unto God, and the Lord called unto him out of the mountain, saying, Thus shalt thou say to the house of Jacob, and tell the children of Israel; . . .' So Milton too will become the inspired spokesman of God before the elect of England. Further, Moses was 'That Shepherd, who first taught the chosen Seed, / In the Beginning how the Heav'ns and Earth / Rose out of *Chaos*': and Milton too will in *Paradise Lost* tell the story of the Creation to 'God's Englishmen'. One must remember the Puritan tendency to identify the English as latter-day Israelites, God's second chosen people: Milton is the neo-Moses and his audience are the neo-Israelites, 'the chosen Seed.' The multiple identifications set up in these lines relate not only to Milton's personal ambitions as poet-prophet but also to the whole context of seventeenth-century religious and political argument.

Before the Children of Israel were established in the promised land, God spoke to them through Moses. Afterwards, God had his permanent sanctuary on the Temple Mount and sent forth his oracle from there in a formalized ritual. Thus the Spirit of God speaks to individuals on the secret tops of mountains, or it may speak to a people in ritualized Temple ceremony; it speaks through prophet or through priest. Milton will assume whichever role the Heav'nly Muse prefers:

> Or if *Sion* Hill
> Delight thee more, and *Siloa's* Brook that flowd
> Fast by the Oracle of God; I thence
> Invoke thy aid . . .

(It is odd to find a biblical scholar such as Milton, who read his Old Testament in the original Hebrew, using Vulgate rather than Hebrew forms of names—'Sion' rather than 'Zion', 'Siloa' rather than 'Shiloach', three-syllabled in the Hebrew; but the preference seems to be purely a matter of sound.) We are again reminded that in *Lycidas* Milton unites in a single person shepherd, poet, prophet and priest. It is interesting that Milton should choose to refer to '*Siloa's* Brook', which is not the most obvious metaphor for the Holy Spirit as established in the Temple. But the spirit of God is often compared in the Old Testament to the refreshing waters of brook or pool, and the waters of Shiloah (this is the Authorized Version form of the name) figure in a variety of biblical contexts as both pool and brook and spring. 'Forsomuch as this people refuseth the waters of Shiloah that go softly,' we read in Isaiah 8:6, and one tradition of biblical exegesis has long taken the waters to stand for the presence of God (though another interprets it as a metaphor for the House of David). We recall, too, such a passage as this from Psalm 46: 'There is a river, the streams whereof shall make glad the city of God, . . . God is in the midst of her' as well as this from Isaiah 33:21: 'But there the glorious Lord will be unto us a place of broad rivers and streams,' and the well-known opening of Psalm 42: 'As the hart panteth after the water brooks, so panteth my soul after thee, O God.' These are, however, only very general echoes. More significant is the fact that Siloach, Siloah, Siloam (it appears in different forms in various places in the Old and the New Testaments) was both a pool situated on the south-west side of the Temple Mount, an artificial channel running through a tunnel hewn in the rock, and a spring on the eastern side of the Mount connected by the channel with the pool. (See Nehemia, 3:4, 'the wall of the pool of Siloah by the king's garden'; John, 9:7: 'Go, wash in the pool of Siloam'.) Milton needed a biblical equivalent of the classical fountains of the Muses, Aganippe and Hippocrene, which were on Mount Helicon. Introducing '*Siloa's* Brook' as a sacred Aganippe, as it were, leads naturally to the comparison between biblical and classical sources of inspiration that follows.

There is no pause as Milton, having invoked the aid of the Heav'nly Muse from whatever source, prophetic or priestly, the Muse prefers, moves on with another relative pronoun to put the Temple Mount above Mount Helicon:

I thence
Invoke thy aid to my adventrous Song,

That with no middle flight intends to soar
Above th' *Aonian* Mount; . . .

Milton has by now introduced four mountains—Horeb, Sinai, the Temple Mount ('*Sion* Hill') and Mount Helicon ('th' *Aonian* Mount'), three biblical to one classical. The Bible is richer in sources of true inspiration than the classics, and Milton needs the richest sources of inspiration he can get, as he intends to soar above Mount Helicon 'with no middle flight' to pursue 'Things unattempted yet in Prose or Rime'. (Does he mean unattempted even in the Bible? Is he going to overgo Moses as Spenser intended to overgo Ariosto? Or does he mean 'unattempted in modern poetry' or 'unattempted in English literature'? Milton is on record as saying that the Bible tells all the truth about ultimate things that men may know or need to know. 'The Scriptures, therefore, partly by reason of their own simplicity, and partly through the divine illumination, are plain and perspicuous in all things necessary to salvation, . . . If then the Scriptures be in themselves so perspicuous, and sufficient of themselves to *make men wise unto salvation through faith*, that *the man of God may be perfect, thoroughly furnished unto all good works*, through what infatuation is it, that even Protestant divines persist in darkening the most momentous truths of religion by intricate metaphysical comments, . . .? As if Scripture, which possesses in itself the clearest light, . . . required to have the simplicity of its divine truths more fully developed, . . .' *Christian Doctrine,* Chapter XXX.) *Paradise Lost* cannot be intended as an explanation of the Bible; it is rather a complete re-telling, under new plenary inspiration deriving from the same divine source as Moses' inspiration, of the whole story of the mutual relations of God and man.)

Having moved from Horeb and Sinai to the Temple Mount, from the prophetic to the priestly environment, Milton feels it necessary to make clear that his inspiration does not really depend on *place* at all; his references to places had the function of establishing his status as poet inspired by God, and now he proceeds to emphasize that the virtuous man is his own Temple and provides his own proper spiritual location:

And chiefly Thou O Spirit, that dost preferr
Before all Temples th' upright heart and pure,
Instruct me, for Thou knowst; . . .

Is he now turning to address someone other than the Heav'nly Muse of line 6? That Muse, as we know from the opening of Book VII, is Urania, originally the Muse of Astronomy (represented bearing a globe, to which she points with a staff) but identified or at least connected in Renaissance literature (e.g. the *Uranie* of Du Bartas) with Solomon's Wisdom, a character in whom Milton was much interested. Addressing Urania in Book VII he says:

> Thou with Eternal wisdom didst converse,
> Wisdom thy Sister, and with her didst play
> In presence of th' Almightie Father, . . .

These lines recall Proverbs 8:30: 'Then I was by him (i.e., God), as one brought up with him: and I was daily his delight, rejoicing always before him' as well as passages in the *Wisdom of Solomon*, and there is no need to follow Saurat in seeing a sexual implication in 'delight' and 'rejoicing' or in Milton's 'didst play'. This is Milton's own rendering of the Hebrew word *sha'eshuim*, which has connotations of playing as of a parent playing with a child. The point is that Milton thought of Wisdom as having some specially intimate relation with God, and Urania, the cosmic divine Muse, as having a specially intimate relation with Wisdom. One might follow this point into endless speculation about Cabalistic and other influences on Milton, but all that is relevant here is to note that Milton first invokes the Heav'nly Muse, associated both with divine wisdom and divine inspiration, the inspirer of Moses on Horeb and Sinai, and then, freeing himself from dependence on place, invokes 'chiefly Thou O Spirit, that dost preferr / Before all Temples th' upright heart and pure'. These are different emanations of the same God—one might even say different metaphors for divine inspiration. He wants now to emphasize the creative aspect of his Muse, so he invokes the Holy Spirit, 'that divine breath or influence by which every thing is created and nourished' (*Christian Doctrine*, Chap. VI). The chapter on the Holy Spirit in *Christian Doctrine* is very relevant here. 'Sometimes it means that impulse or voice of God by which the prophets were inspired. Sometimes it means that light of truth, whether ordinary or extraordinary, wherewith God enlightens and leads his people' (*C.D.* VI). So Milton appeals: 'What in me is dark /

Illumin . . .' The term Holy Spirit 'is also used to signify the spiritual gifts conferred by God on individuals, and the act of gift itself'.

The appeal in lines 17–23 combines humility and enormous self-confidence. The humility is evidenced by the very fact that Milton makes the appeal, and by the quiet, rocking motion of

> What in me is dark
> Illumin, what is low raise and support; . . .

The self-confidence comes from Milton's implicit identification of himself with the ideal character described in Psalm 15: 'Lord, who shall abide in thy tabernacle? who shall dwell in thy holy hill? He that walketh uprightly, and worketh righteousness, and speaketh the truth in his heart.' '*Sion* Hill' becomes now a state of mind and soul, not a physical place. 'Who shall dwell in thy holy hill?' asks the Psalmist, and the answer is determined not by where a man is but by what he is. Milton has subsumed all the holy mountains in the 'holy hill' of the Psalmist, which is a metaphor for the virtuous character. I might add that it is not in the least extravagant to insist that Milton expected his readers to have this Psalm in mind when reading his lines: he wrote for a public that knew much of the Bible by heart, and these lines clearly refer to this Psalm. Indeed, it cannot be too often emphasized what an important part in the reverberating spirals of meaning is played throughout *Paradise Lost* by implicit appeals to both biblical and classical echoes: these appeals were part of the strength of the English poetic language as Milton knew it, and to read Milton without being aware of them is to hear his words with much of their poetic meaning strained out.

The Spirit to whom Milton appeals in this final and climactic part of his introduction is a Spirit available only to very specially endowed persons. 'Thirdly, the Spirit signifies a divine impulse, or light, or voice, or word, transmitted from above either through Christ, who is the Word of God, or by some other channel (*C.D.* II)." Milton is here claiming to be 'some other channel', comparable in some ways to Christ himself, yet at the same time in need of help and instruction. 'Instruct me, for Thou know'st.' The appeal moves on with rising eloquence to appeal to the Spirit as the creative element in God:

> Thou from the first
> Wast present, and with mighty wings outspred
> Dove-like satst brooding on the vast Abyss
> And mad'st it pregnant: . . .

'In the beginning God created the heaven and the earth. And the earth was without form, and void; and darkness was upon the face of the deep. And the Spirit of God moved upon the face of the waters' (Genesis 1:1–2). The Spirit of God which moved upon the face of the waters at the creation (or, according to Milton's explanation in *C.D.*, VII, immediately *after* the creation of heaven and earth) is the same Spirit that John saw in the form of a dove: 'And John bare record, saying, I saw the Spirit descending from heaven like a dove, and it abode upon him' (John, 1:32). Milton comments in *C.D.*, VI: 'Further, the Spirit signifies the person itself of the Holy Spirit, or its symbol. John i. 32, 33 "like a dove". Nor let it be objected, that a dove is not a person; for an intelligent substance, under any form whatever, is a person; . . .' It seems clear that in lines 20–22 Milton, in spite of his remark in *C.D.* that the Spirit moved on the waters only after the creation, is accepting the tradition that the Spirit created the world by 'hatching it out', bird-like, in 'brooding on the vast Abyss'. The word translated simply as 'moved' in the Authorized Version, the Hebrew *merachepeth*, has the sense of hovering over or brooding over, a meaning discussed at length by many patristic and mediaeval Jewish commentators with whom Milton was familiar. One patristic rendering of the word is actually *incubabat*, while the mediaeval Jewish commentator Solomon ben Isaac (Rashi) explains that the Throne of Glory was suspended in the air, hovering over the waters, sustained by the breath (or spirit—the Hebrew word is the same) of God and His command, like a dove hovering over the nest. Talking of 'the Spirit of God, the fire and scintillation of that noble and mighty Essence', Sir Thomas Browne in *Religio Medici* remarks: 'This is that gentle heat that brooded on the waters, and in six days hatched the World; . . .' and in Vaughan's poem *The Water-fall* there occur the lines

> . . . Unless that Spirit lead his minde,
> Which first upon thy face did move,
> And hatch'd all with his quickning love.

Milton is thus taking an established tradition of the Spirit of God brooding over the waters at the creation and associating it with the poet brooding over his material in the process of poetic creation. The poet has been linked with shepherd, with prophet, with priest, and with the perfect man of Psalm 15: now he is linked by analogy to God Himself. Just as God created the world through the brooding and hatching of His Holy Spirit, so Milton asks that same Spirit to assist him in *his* creative process,

> That to the highth of this great Argument
> I may assert Eternal Providence,
> And justifie the wayes of God to men.

There is a steady progression here, a steady rising in the status of the rôle played by the poet, from the private individual finding his own inspiration from God 'on the secret top' of a mountain to the public defender of Providence declaiming his 'great Argument'. The greater vibrancy of utterance in the final three lines of the introduction, where the words move on with no pause within the line to achieve a climax of eloquence, is thus closely linked to the movement of thought.

There is also a progression from the general to the particular, from large elemental terms to specific, particular terms. The opening lines are full of simple, elemental words—Man, Fruit, Tree, Death, World. This is the first and largest statement of the theme. (Yet even here we notice that he appeals with a certain intimacy to his readers' knowledge of biblical story—'Of *that* Forbidden Tree'—in the same way, as I have noted above, that he does in referring to Moses as 'That Shepherd'.) Milton then proceeds to particularize individual places (—Oreb, Sinai, Sion Hill, Siloa's Brook, th' Aonian Mount. Finally, he comes to himself—'I thence / Invoke thy aid . . .'; 'Instruct me, . . .' 'What in me is dark / Illumin, . . .'; 'That . . . I may assert . . .' We begin by confronting the theme and we end with the poet rising before us in his creative majesty. The delayed entry of the 'I' carries a significance that is not found in the casual initial use of the first person in 'Arma virumque cano' or Ἄνδρα μοι ἔννεπε, μοῦσα.

In the whole of these twenty-six lines there are only seven which have no internal pause at all. The first of these is line 13,

Invoke thy aid to my adventrous Song,

which moves on steadily as though to emphasize the poet's determination to soar upward unhindered. This sense is emphasized in the following line, which also contains no pause,

That with no middle flight intends to soar.

The daring finality of line 16 is emphasized by the lack of pause:

Things unattempted yet in Prose or Rime,

Line 18 may be said to have no pause, though there is a slight pause after 'Temples' and there is no sense of relentless march. Line 21, which certainly contains no internal pause, achieves by its steadiness the feeling of brooding conveyed by the sense:

Dove-like satst brooding on the vast Abyss.

The remaining three lines with no internal pause are the last three of the introduction, with the emphatic and climactic effect already discussed. All the other lines have internal pauses varied in order to achieve particular effects. The whole twenty-six lines constitute a remarkable piece of verbal orchestration, ending with the massive chords of

And justifie the wayes of God to men.

Then there comes at least a bar's rest (to continue the musical analogy) before a much more lightly orchestrated passage (shall we say, simply a group of woodwinds?) opens the poem proper:

Say first, for Heav'n hides nothing from thy view . . .

But the sound steadily thickens, until in line 34 the drums roll with the introduction to 'Th' infernal Serpent'.

It is not difficult to discuss Milton's sound patterns and his handling of verbal cadence. The temptation succumbed to by so many earlier critics has been to produce such analyses divorced from any but the most perfunctory discussion of the intellectual-emotional texture of the language. That texture is carefully wrought, and to see it for what it really is we must be aware both of the ways in which Milton shared background knowledge with his readers by his deliberate manipulation of suggestive echoes and of the ways in which he posed himself, as it were, with reference both to his material and to his audience.

V

SYNTAX AND MUSIC IN *PARADISE LOST*

Donald Davie

I

NO LINES from *Paradise Lost* are more familiar than those near the beginning of the first Book which describe the fall of Satan from heaven:

> Him the Almighty Power
> Hurld headlong flaming from th' Ethereal Skie,
> With hideous ruin and combustion down
> To bottomless perdition, there to dwell
> In Adamantine Chains and penal Fire,
> Who durst defie th' Omnipotent to Arms.
>
> (i. 44–9)

'Dramatic' is a poor word for this effect. One wants instead to speak of 'muscularity', using 'muscular', however, in a special sense, different from (because more literal than) the sense in which we can justly speak of other poetry as 'muscular'. The effect is kinetic. The placing of 'Him', 'down' and 'To', in particular, gives us the illusion as we read that our own muscles are tightening in panic as we experience in our own bodies a movement just as headlong and precipitate as the one described. We occupy in ourselves the *gestalt* of the falling, just as we do before a good painting of the same event; it is hardly too much to say that the inversion of word-order (object-subject-verb) has the same effect upon us as seeing the angel's head near the bottom of the painted canvas and his heels near the top.

Because the literally unimaginable nature of his subject prevented Milton from appealing at all often or consistently to our visualizing faculty, he finds an especially valuable compensation for this whenever he can thus appeal to the reader's kinetic sense. Another example of this—again a well-known passage—comes in the course of Satan's flight through Chaos:

> Quencht in a Boggie *Syrtis*, neither Sea
> Nor good dry Land: nigh founderd on he fares,
> Treading the crude consistence, half on foot,
> Half flying; behoves him now both Oar and Sail.
> As when a Gryfon through the Wilderness
> With winged course ore Hill or moarie Dale,
> Persues the *Arimaspian*, who by stelth
> Had from his wakeful custody purloind
> The guarded Gold: So eagerly the Fiend
> Ore bog or steep, through strait, rough, dense or rare,
> With head, hands, wings or feet persues his way,
> And swims or sinks, or wades, or creeps, or flies.
> (ii. 939–50)

From Milton's own day, when some of his contemporaries essayed the same effect before him (with less tact), there have always been those to admire the way in which—with 'strait, rough, dense', and 'head, hands, wings'—Milton crowds stressed syllables together so as to make the vocal exertion in reading image the physical exertion described. It is the reader, too, who flounders, stumbles, pushes doggedly on. Just as skilful, though less conspicuous, is the way in which line-break, punctuation and metre combine to make 'Half flying' act out, in our speaking of the words, the abbreviated and ungainly flap which they describe.

Though dramatic is an inadequate word, it is still the right word for these felicities, because what they do is to force us to participate in the situation and the actions described; we no longer merely observe these, in imagination we suffer them, ourselves embroiled. This point is worth making, because elsewhere Milton uses the same elements—metre played off against syntax and word-order—to quite different effects, no less fine, which I would call rather 'narrative' than 'dramatic'. I have in mind the invocation to Light at the beginning of Book III:

> thee I revisit safe,
> And feel thy sovran vital Lamp; but thou
> Revisitst not these eyes, that roul in vain
> To find thy piercing ray, and find no dawn;
> So thick a drop serene hath quencht thir Orbs,
> Or dim suffusion veild. Yet not the more
> Cease I to wander where the Muses haunt
> Clear Spring, or shadie Grove, or Sunnie Hill,
> Smit with the love of sacred song; but chief
> Thee *Sion* and the flowrie Brooks beneath
> That wash thy hallowd feet, and warbling flow,
> Nightly I visit: nor somtimes forget
> Those other two equald with me in Fate,
> So were I equald with them in renown,
> Blind *Thamyris* and blind *Maeonides*,
> And *Tiresias* and *Phineus* Prophets old.
> Then feed on thoughts, that voluntarie move
> Harmonious numbers; as the wakeful Bird
> Sings darkling, and in shadiest Covert hid,
> Tunes her nocturnal Note. Thus with the Year
> Seasons return, but not to me returns
> Day, or the sweet approach of Ev'n or Morn
> Or sight of vernal bloom, or Summers Rose,
> Or flocks, or herds, or human face divine;
> But cloud in stead, and ever-during dark
> Surrounds me, from the cheerful ways of men
> Cut off, and for the Book of knowledge fair
> Presented with a Universal blanc
> Of Natures works to mee expung'd and ras'd,
> And wisdom at one entrance quite shut out.
>
> (iii. 21–50)

It seems absurd, in order to illustrate a narrative effect, to take from a narrative poem precisely that passage (an invocation) by which the narrative is interrupted. Yet the distinction of this passage, in all which concerns the manipulation of syntax (and the syntax is profoundly important) is thoroughly a narrative distinction. The language is deployed, just as the episodes are in a story, so as always to provoke the question 'And then?'—to provoke this question and to answer it in unexpected ways. If any arrangement of language is a sequence of verbal events, here syntax is employed so as to make the most of each word's eventfulness, so as to make each key-word, like each new episode in a well told story, at once surprising and just. The eventfulness of language comes out for instance in 'Then feed on thoughts that voluntarie move', where at the line-ending 'move' seems intransitive, and as such wholly satisfying; until the swing on to the next line, 'Harmonious numbers', reveals it (a little surprise, but a wholly fair one) as transitive. This flicker of hesitation about whether the thoughts move only themselves, or something else, makes us see that the numbers aren't really 'something else' but are the very thoughts themselves, seen under a new aspect; the placing of 'move', which produces the momentary uncertainty about its grammar, ties together 'thoughts' and 'numbers' in a relation far closer than cause and effect. Or again, how eventful is 'Day' at the start of line 42! The inversion, 'not to me returns' has forged for the long-awaited subject of 'returns' a link every bit as strong as rhyme, with 'Seasons', in the corresponding place in the line above, and in the same grammatical relation to the identical verb 'return'. Thus, what we expect is a word parallel in meaning, just as it is parallel in metrical placement and grammatical function. We expect 'Spring'. What we get is 'Day'. And this is surprising. Yet the surprise is no cheap or empty one, for the parallel in meaning is in fact better enforced by 'Day' than by 'Spring' which, we now see, would have been lamely predictable. The surprisingness of 'Day' isolates it for our attention so that we take the force of its double meaning as at once a division of time and a synonym for 'light'. Similarly, we might notice how the virtuosity of the grammatical construction 'nor somtimes forget . . . So were I' works with the metrical arrangement to clamp together 'Fate' and 'renown' in a relationship which is not rhyme but is altogether as close and satisfying as if it were.

Given a syntax as elaborate as Milton's, the variety of effects is endless. Yet all depend equally, at bottom, on provoking and answering the simple narrative question, 'What happens next?' They all become possible only with the recognition, by poet and reader alike, that language and therefore the arts of language operate through and over spans of time, in terms of successive events, each new sentence a new small action with its own sometimes complicated plot. It is a perception about language which much of the most influential modern criticism—working as it does through spatial metaphors, talking of 'the figure in the carpet', of tensions balanced and cancelling out inside structures —seems expressly designed to obscure. This occupying of a duration, of a lapse of time, is what connects the literary arts, but especially poetry, with the art of music, which works through time in the same way. And as, to image the very different effect of the lines on Satan's fall we found an analogy with painting, so to explain effects of this sort our analogies would need to be from music, just because of that central principle of music which Milton himself isolated when he spoke of 'linked sweetness long drawn out'. There is no need to take account of the various sonorities of the invocation to Light, in order to establish that it is exquisitely musical. As in Spenser's marriage-hymns, which may have been Milton's exemplary model for this sort of writing, the music is first and foremost in the structure, metrical and syntactical; it is the way the syntactical units are draped across the line-endings, the playing off of syntactical pause against metrical pause, the varying of word-order and clause-order, which give the centrally musical effect of never stopping but to start again. And all this is logically, as well as (I think) in the experience of reading, prior to the tone-colouring of vowels that are long or short, dark or light, open or closed, and the various combinations of liquid and fricative in consonantal clusters.

II

Reading the note on 'The Verse', prefixed to the *Paradise Lost* of 1668, we learn, of 'true musical delight', that it consists, for Milton, 'only in apt Numbers, fit quantity of syllables, and the sense variously drawn out from one Verse into another'. That last phrase, if we hear it echo 'linked sweetness long drawn out', will have prepared us for just such effects as those of the invocation to Light. What is surprising is that these effects are rather the exception than the rule. Neither kinetic and dramatic effect, as in the lines on Satan's fall, nor narrative and musical effect, as in the invocation to Light, are in evidence at all frequently as we read *Paradise Lost*. For example:

> Others with vast *Typhœan* rage more fell
> Rend up both Rocks and Hills, and ride the Air
> In whirlwind; Hell scarce holds the wild uproar.
> As when *Alcides* from *Œchalia* Crownd
> With conquest, felt th' envenomd robe, and tore
> Through pain up by the roots *Thessalian* Pines,
> And *Lichas* from the top of *Œta* threw
> Into th' *Euboic* Sea.
>
> (ii. 539–46)

Or, more strikingly:

> Th' undaunted Fiend what this might be admir'd,
> Admir'd, not fear'd; God and his Son except,
> Created thing naught valu'd he nor shunnd;
> And with disdainful look thus first began.
>
> (ii. 677–80)

In these passages, the point is not that some of the lines are end-stopped—both 'uproar' in the first, for instance, and 'shunnd' in the second, ending a parenthesis with the end of a line—but that where the line is not end-stopped, the swing of the reading eye or voice around the line-ending is not turned to poetically expressive use. Certainly this happens with lines 539 and 540, where we swing around the line-ending to come hard upon the energetic verb, 'Rend'. But there is no expressive or dramatic reason why 'Air' should be separated in this way from 'In whirlwind'—a phrase which merely dangles limply into the next line. More remarkably, in lines 543 and 544, the interposition of 'Through pain' precludes both of two possible dramatic effects—either the violence of 'Tore' at the beginning of the line, or the even more effective muscularity of having 'tore' separated by the line-ending from 'Up'. Similarly, in the last two lines of the first passage the Latinate inversion of word-order means that as we launch out from 'threw' into the last line, we are asking not '*What* was thrown?' but only the much less interesting question 'thrown where?' In fact, this question is so unexciting that we don't even ask it; so that 'Into th' *Euboic* Sea' hangs superfluous —the sentence could just as well have ended where the line ends, after 'threw'. As for the second passage, the line-endings are so far from being dramatically significant that Milton seems to have gone perversely out of his way to eliminate all that might be suspenseful. Inversion of word-order answers the question of what the Fiend 'admir'd', before we have the chance to ask it. If we had been made to wait for the object of 'admir'd' until after admiration had been distinguished from fear and the distinction elaborated on, a powerful suspense would have been built up. Instead the narrative run is halted while the distinction is laboriously made in a parenthesis which has all the distracting inertness of a footnote.

It's impossible, with this second passage, to think that Milton has simply muffed his chances. We have to suppose that the arrangement is deliberate: that the sort of suspense and eventfulness we are asking for is something that Milton as a general rule won't give; that the expressiveness of the syntax in the invocation to Light is exceptional. And the implication is plain: if the distinction between admiration and fear is, as Milton conveys it, a sort of footnote, then this is a sort of poem in which the footnotes matter more than the text. The story, the narrative, is only a convenient skeleton; its function is to provoke interesting and important speculative questions. Or rather, the story told is centrally important to Milton precisely because it does raise (and, so Milton would claim, it answers) all these questions, all the questions worth asking. But the story told is not important as a story *in the telling*, as narrative, as provoking and then resolving suspense; it does not invite the questions, 'What happened next?' or 'This happened—yes, to whom?'

It would obviously be wrong to say that in *Paradise Lost* there is no element of suspense at all, nothing to keep the mind as well as the ear reaching forward from one paragraph to the next. For instance, a reasonably instructed reader of Satan's encounter at Hell Gate with Sin and Death will note the emblematic, riddling quality in the images of the two mysterious shapes either side of the gate, and will reach forward in an interested suspense to the point at which the riddle is explained and the shapes are named.

Allegory shows how this can become a truly narrative interest, making the emblem reveal its rubric, the riddle its own solution, in one seamless process:

> But, full of fire and greedy hardiment,
> The youthfull Knight could not for ought be staide;
> But forth unto the darksom hole he went,
> And looked in: his glistring armour made
> A little glooming light, much like a shade;
> By which he saw the ugly monster plaine,
> Halfe like a serpent horribly displaide,
> But th'other halfe did woman's shape retaine
> Most lothsom, filthie, foule, and full of vile disdaine.
>
> And, as she lay upon the durtie ground,
> Her huge long taile her den all overspred,
> Yet was in knots and many boughtes upwound,
> Pointed with mortall sting. Of her there bred
> A thousand young ones, which she dayly fed,
> Sucking upon her poisnous dugs; each one
> Of sundrie shapes, yet all ill-favored:
> Soone as that uncouth light upon them shone,
> Into her mouth they crept, and suddain all were gone.

In the first of these famous stanzas from the first canto of 'The Faerie Queene', the last line ('Most lothsom, filthie, foule, and full of vile disdaine') is the sort of slack wordiness in Spenser, and in the Elizabethans generally, which we cannot justify but have to put up with for the sake of other things. Apart from this, the passage is continuously alive with narrative interest. In the long last line of the second stanza, for instance, the extra foot is turned to brilliant use. It enables Spenser to break the line into equal halves, and then make the second half accelerate away from the first. The line slows to a halt on 'crept', and then, with 'suddain', jumps off rapidly from the comma. 'And suddain all were gone'—the dragon's brood, just now moving sluggishly to their haven, all at once reach it in a flash.

Spenser's passage was certainly in Milton's mind when he created the image of Sin:

> Before the Gates there sat
> On either side a formidable shape;
> The one seemd Woman to the waist, and fair,
> But ended foul in many a scaly fold
> Voluminous and vast, a Serpent armd
> With mortal sting: about her middle round
> A cry of Hell Hounds never ceasing barkd
> With wide *Cerberean* mouths full loud, and rung
> A hideous Peal; yet, when they list, would creep,
> If aught disturbd thir noise, into her womb,
> And kennel there, yet there still barkd and howld
> Within unseen.
>
> (ii. 648–59)

We cannot say that Milton's puppies disappear at a steady pace where Spenser's little reptiles go with a rush. The truth is that the manner of their creeping, the act of it, has not been experienced by Milton, as so clearly it was by Spenser. This is not to say just that Milton hasn't *seen* the incident, though as usual he hasn't, where Spenser plainly has, though his image is just as hard for the mind's eye to grasp. But there are more ways of experiencing than through the eye. Through the ear, for instance; but Milton's hell-hounds just bark and bark unchangingly, from first to last. In Spenser's 'pointed with mortall sting', the 'point' is not seen but felt. (There's a similar tactile effect in Spenser's 'knots' and 'many boughtes'; Milton's equivalent, 'voluminous and vast' has nothing to recommend it but alliterative sonority.) By contrast, Milton's 'armed / With mortal sting' isn't *experienced* at all; 'armed' represents a high degree of abstraction from any sense-experience. And if the abstractness is confirmed on the one hand by the highly intellectual wit of 'kennel', on the other it produces 'fair' ponderously and needlessly opposed to 'foul'.

Of course this intellectuality of *Paradise Lost*, the absence from it of any immediacy of sense-impression, is an old story. Yet it influences everything else. In the episode at Hell's Gate for instance, as soon as Milton sets one of his Shapes in motion, the shape of Death ('If shape it might be calld that shape had none /

Distinguishable in member, joint or limb'), one sees at once how impossible it was for him to enact in syntax across line-division the manner of Death's moving, as Spenser enacts in a slightly later stanza the wreathing leap of his dragon on to the knight's shield. Such enactment cannot take place, since Milton no more than anyone else can explain how Death takes 'horrid strides' when it isn't clear whether Death has legs.

What's most noticeable, however, is how Milton does not avail himself of the narrative interest of allegory. When Spenser describes Error's brood as 'each one / Of sundrie shapes, yet all ill-favored', he is enriching at one and the same time the literal image and the allegorical. The allegorical significance is artfully thus uncovered, gradually, in a way to answer the narrative question 'What next?' Milton, on the other hand, proceeds through two distinct stages—first, the enigmatic image, and then, a hundred lines later, the solution to the enigma, the explanation of how Sin got to be the way she is.

III

There is evidence that in the present age those readers who still take pleasure in *Paradise Lost* sometimes do so by regarding it, not primarily as a narrative (epic or heroic poem), but rather as a poetic encyclopaedia of arcane knowledge, of ardent and curious speculation. This seems to be, for instance, the drift of J. B. Broadbent's insistence:

> 'Milton's material is not only integrated at every point with his poem's plot, but was a matter of living interest to all educated people at the time of writing. One can only say that to the seventeenth century China, vultures, Ganges, etc., were what the prehistoric past was to the Victorians and what space-satellites and abominable snowmen are to us.'[1]

It is doubtless easy to present this sort of reading of *Paradise Lost*

[1] J. B. Broadbent, 'Milton and Arnold'. *Essays in Criticism VI*.4. (October, 1956), p. 411.

as an evasion, by a secularized century, of the theological challenge carried in the myth-story conceived as literally true. And of course it is obvious that to a non-Christian or tepidly Christian reader of the present day some such shift must take place. Yet an examination of the syntax of the poem suggests that this sort of interest was invited by Milton from the first; especially as we read on after the first two books, we encounter more and more cases in which the narrative is quite abruptly halted in order to indulge and invite speculations (often theological, of course, as well as geographical, cosmological and scientific).

For this frustration of the narrative interest can be seen in other ways and on a much larger scale than in the manipulations of syntax by which inverted word-order answers our interesting questions before we have time to ask them. Milton continually disrupts his narrative's present time, by looking into the future. When Satan confronts Death—

> so matcht they stood;
> For never but once more was either like
> To meet so great a foe.
>
> (ii. 720–22)

When he launches out through Chaos—

> So he with difficulty and labour hard
> Mov'd on, with difficulty and labour he;
> But hee once past, soon after when Man fell,
> Strange alteration! Sin and Death amain
> Following his track, such was the will of Heav'n,
> Pav'd after him a broad and beaten way
> Over the dark Abyss, whose boiling Gulf
> Tamely endur'd a Bridge of wondrous length. . . .
>
> (ii. 1021–28)

(Here the characteristic repetition of 'with difficulty and labour' reveals—as nearly all such cases must—a refusal to profit by syntactical resources, so as to weave the anticipation into the narrative. Milton prefers to halt the narrative and disrupt the narrative time.) Continually, before the Fall has happened, we are made to look forward to what will be when it has. Merely a reference to 'Amarant' is enough to provoke this (iii. 352–59). Or a few lines later, when Satan first alights from Chaos:

> So on this windie Sea of Land, the Fiend
> Walkd up and down alone bent on his prey,
> Alone, for other Creature in this place
> Living or liveless to be found was none,
> None yet, but store hereafter from the earth . . .
> (iii. 440–44)

And so we are thrust out of the narrative present into this 'hereafter', into what in the story hasn't yet come to pass, to hear a long account of the Paradise of Fools. This sort of thing crops up too consistently, every few pages or so, not to be deliberately contrived. It might be justified as an instance of the so-called 'figural' realism of mediaeval drama, which is similarly lordly about the chronology of sacred events.[1] But because the overt structure of *Paradise Lost* is narrative, and because of the speculative learning encrusted upon its every angle, this consistent disrupting of the present time inevitably distracts the reader's attention from the poem as narrative to the poem as encyclopaedia.

This was the point at issue when John Peter quarrelled with Sir Herbert Grierson about 'Tears such as angels weep'. Sir Herbert had applauded (in his *Milton and Wordsworth*, p. 107):

> 'that tremendous stroke which one might hardly have expected from Milton, Satan shaken with remorse as he surveys the fallen followers of his pride:
>
> "Thrice he essay'd, and thrice in spite of scorn
> Tears such as angels weep burst forth; at last
> Words interwoven with sighs found out their way"'

And he asked, 'Is there even in Shakespeare a greater moment?' John Peter, taking up the challenge, set beside these lines a passage from *Coriolanus* and another from *King Lear*, and remarked:

[1] Erich Auerbach, *Mimesis*, tr. Willard Trask. Princeton University Press, 1953. (pp. 156–8).

> 'Someone may indeed point to "Tears such as angels weep" as being in its way an equivalent for these Shakespearean effects . . . but will such a claim bear examination? Sir Herbert himself does seem to assume that the phrase is a touch of sublimity and that Milton wants us to feel how precious celestial tears must be. But if we had been through the poem once we should know how frequently Milton strays from his main themes to tell us about the substance and properties of angels and we might well feel that these words contained only a simple prosaic qualification—"the tears that angels, like men, can weep (for they can)" rather than "celestial tears". Thus if in fact we were re-reading the poem we might on the one hand have the advantage of seeing Satan's weeping as a striking variation from his habitual demeanour but on the other hand our reaction to the phrase describing his tears would almost certainly be much cooler and less immediate than Sir Herbert would appear to allow. The definitional sense of the phrase would have shrivelled its connotations of sublimity and we should be able to see how little there is in common between it and the other simile in Coriolanus'.[1]

One may believe that Mr. Peter read the phrase aright, where Sir Herbert Grierson didn't, and agree that it is indeed used to define. But is this, then, so uninteresting? Mr. Peter's 'shrivelled' is a very strong word. Is defining so poor a thing in poetry, as opposed to 'connotations', that words used for denotation can appear only as the shrivelled husk of what could have been, and *should* have been, evocative of reverberations? What we have, Mr. Peter says, is 'only a simple prosaic qualification'. But why 'only'? In short, the point is well made that in the past admirers of Milton have often praised him for the wrong reasons. But it is still possible to admire him on quite different grounds, in the way hinted at, for instance, by J. B. Broadbent. Stressing the encyclopaedic interest of the poem, Mr. Broadbent speaks also of its

[1] John Peter, 'Reflections on the Milton Controversy'. *Scrutiny, XIX*, 1., pp. 10–11. The lines from Coriolanus are:

> 'If you have writ your annals true, 'tis there,
> That, like an eagle in a dove-cote, I
> Flutter'd your Volscians in Corioli:
> Alone I did it.'

'textural stiffness', and describes its diction as 'stiff, pedantic and exact'. We seem to be in sight of a prosaic *Paradise Lost*, and prepared perhaps to endorse Hazlitt's striking judgement: 'That approximation to the severity of impassioned prose which has been made an objection to Milton's poetry . . . is one of its greatest excellences.'

To all this, however, there is one great objection. What happens, on this showing, to Milton's notorious 'organ-music'? To come at it another way, the difficulty with any poem that is 'encyclopaedic' is how its encyclopaedic speculations are to be bound together into one whole. Mr. Broadbent anticipates this when he says that 'Milton's material is . . . integrated at every point with his poem's plot'. But we have seen that Milton often deploys his 'plot', the action of his story, in such a way as to frustrate our interest in it. And this means that the developing plot cannot, as we read the poem, hold together the massive and various learning it is made to carry; the unity imposed by the plot is only schematic, it is not felt by the reader as a central interest driving through. What is more, if the unifying structure of the poem is thus not a narrative structure, by the same token it cannot be musical. For music operates, just as narrative does, by provoking and then resolving suspense about 'What next?' And Milton characteristically frustrates this sort of interest, as much in his plotting of the movement through narrated episodes as in his plotting of the movement from word to word, from clause to clause, through a sentence. This means that by and large the famous music cannot be a structural principle, as it is in the invocation to Light, leading on the reader's lively interest from line to line; rather it is a matter of vocal colouring and skilful resonance, leading only the voice and the ear. And this, surely, is what our experience tells us, when we read the poem. The 'musical delight' is all in sonority, not at all in movement forward, through suspense to resolution and a new suspense. Dr. Leavis's account of this Miltonic music (there are other musics, in other poems) seems more clearly just on each new reading. And so it appears that the splendidly elaborate syntax, which one could suppose created precisely as a musical resource, which indeed proves itself such a resource in a passage like the invocation to Light, in fact is employed characteristically to check narrative impetus and frustrate musical pleasure. Milton's composition—

taken sentence by sentence as well as book by book—may indeed be, in the time-honoured phrase, 'architectural'. From one point of view this is only to emphasize that it cannot be musical; that *Paradise Lost*, in the reading, never or hardly ever profits by what is a fact about it as about any poem—that it exists as a shape cut in time.

VI

ADAM UNPARADISED

Frank Kermode

Molto è licito là, che qui non lece
alle nostre virtù, mercè del loco
fatto per proprio dell'umana spece.

NO LONGER is it fashionable to use Raleigh's famous phrase, and call *Paradise Lost* a monument to dead ideas; but some such assumption underlies much of the modern hostility to Milton, however well-concealed it may be. The proper answer to the charge is not that the ideas are, on the contrary, alive; but that the poem is not a monument to *any* ideas. And only an answer of that kind has much chance of being heard. The poem has had many ingenious and scholarly defenders; they have explained the habits of seventeenth-century readers, and shown that Milton was precise where he has been accused of imprecision; they have said a good deal about the poet's theology and even argued that literate Christians find no difficulty at all with his ideas. It is very good to have all this information; but it will not touch the quick of the objectors' position. No writer, so far as I know, has come so near to explaining what this is as the late A. J. A. Waldock did when he argued that the modern reader is really much too expert in fiction to put up with the crudity of Milton's narrative, and his imperfect control of its tone.[1] It is perfectly true that the modern reader, who thinks of novels when he thinks of long narratives, and who thinks of novels in post-Jamesian terms, will not find Milton 'thinking with his story' in the modern way; and he may

[1] A. J. A. Waldock, *Paradise Lost and its Critics* (1947).

assume that the reason for this failure is that Milton's mind was, on a great many points, made up for him in advance. And Waldock finds a damaging conflict between the official significance of what happens, and the natural bent of the narrative. This is held to limit the poem, to prevent its being what Lascelles Abercrombie nobly said epic poetry ought to be, an exhibition of 'life in some great symbolic attitude'.[1] I myself think this phrase precisely appropriate to *Paradise Lost*, and in a sense what I have to say is an indirect answer to Waldock. In fact, modern reader as I am, I find *Paradise Lost* wonderfully satisfying; not because of an odd taste for verses which have the qualities called by the Greek critic magnificence, sweetness and gravity, but because Milton's poem seems to me enduringly to represent, or better to embody, life in a great symbolic attitude.

The Naïve

It is after all perverse of the modern reader to affect distaste at Milton's dependence on naïve materials; he ought to be properly conditioned to their use in art, not only by certain books of prime importance to him, but by the force of the whole Romantic tradition, which always worshipped the primitive and became very explicit about the cult long before the end of the last century. It is to be studied anywhere from Herder to Nietzsche and Cassirer, from Rousseau to Jung, from Wordsworth to Pound; and when Gilbert Murray said that 'for full mental health the channels between primitive and sophisticated must be kept open' he spoke not only for a group of Cambridge scholars but for everybody. If there is one paramount requirement for major modern literature, it is that it should have a 'naïve' topic; that it should have found its myth; for only thus can everything be got in, and the whole truth presented, which would, under the conditions of sophisticated discourse, merely rattle endlessly on. So Mr. Eliot, with *Ulysses* in mind, spoke of myth as 'a way of controlling, of ordering, of giving a shape and a significance to the immense panorama of futility and anarchy which is contemporary history'; and Mr. Forster refers to the artist's power to do this as 'love', the power that can 'keep thought out'.

Yet the world that these works confront is neither controlled by love nor free of 'thought'; and thought concerns itself, in

[1] *The Epic* (n.d.), p. 56.

A Passage to India and in *The Waste Land* as well as in *Paradise Lost*, with the conditions created by love's absence or corruption. There is a myth at the root of the work, and it contains all possible explanations; but the poem has to make it new and make it relevant. As much as any 'barren philosphy precept'—to adapt Greville's expression—it must be turned into 'pregnant images of life', whether it is the Grail or Paradise. The truth of the poem depends upon this process, not upon the special power of its theme. The modern reader has to agree not to indulge a special disrespect for Milton's myth; he should not despise it more than any other that accounts for the origin of death; but he must not be asked, on the other hand, to have a special respect for it, or for Milton's theology or his epic style. He owes them no more than he owes the story or the Hindu theology of *A Passage to India*, though of course he owes them no less.

Here, perhaps we arrive at an obstacle; it may appear that there is some confidence trick to be on one's guard against. Admirers of Milton do not often use the word 'myth' in this connection, or offer full (though not licentious) freedom of interpretation. It may be that Waldock himself, having claimed this liberty, was afraid to use it; for he seems to call the poem wrong wherever he finds it pulling against what he assumes to be Milton's intention. It is important that one should be clear at this point, and understand that there is nothing in Milton's myth, nor in his own attitude to it so far as we can know what that was, to forbid the degree of liberty here proposed.

Bible Truth

As Johnson saw, Milton 'chose a subject on which too much could not be said'. Already in its primitive form it showed life in a symbolic attitude; to exhaust its implications you would have to say everything about everything. Of its nature, indeed, it would appear differently to different men, and to the same man at different times, so that no one man could ever say enough about it. A great many men had already had their say, and Milton knew a lot about his predecessors, and about the wide differences in their opinions as to the significance of the biblical narrative in later times.

A society whose sacred book is primitive closes the gap time has made by various devices of sophisticated explanation, of which allegory is the most important; with it the Stoics built a bridge between Homer and themselves, and generations of exegetes brought the Old Testament into conformity with a contemporary view of life.[1] Milton, though he is sparing of allegory, naturally had to think of his subject in something like this way, and obviously supposed that whatever the inconsistencies and difficulties it presented to a modern poet—many of them were as clear to him as to his commentators—this myth, precisely because of its inclusive quality, its containing the truth in little, could certainly be established as fully relevant to the here and now. Longinus said of certain parts of Homer that they were utterly indecorous unless taken allegorically; Milton has to stretch his literalism beyond breaking point to accept the Bible when it says that God laughed or repented (*De Doctrina Christiana* I. ii); and for all that he found the Bible 'plain and perspicuous in all things necessary to salvation' he also held that it accommodated itself to the needs of its readers, 'even of the most unlearned' (*De Doctrina Christiana* I. xxx). A perception of allegory or of 'accommodation' is the prelude to a certain liberty of interpreting, however restrained.

With a tradition of various interpretations behind him, all assuming that this myth embodied the whole human condition and could accordingly be endlessly explicated, Milton, though respecting the actual text of Genesis, thought himself entitled to handle it with a certain freedom, precisely in order to establish its universality. He would not have liked the word 'myth', at any rate in the sense here used; yet he does, in a way, treat his central topic rather as he does all those other related myths, mostly classical, which he is always bringing in. There is the important difference that these are usually rejected as erroneous fictions; but what makes them worth mentioning is that they contain (though only by natural light) ancient wisdom, worth remembering, recording, and correcting. It is curious that Cowley, a pioneer whom Milton admired, had a decade earlier pronounced the whole repertory of classical myth to be exhausted; Milton suggests, with far more delicacy, and in the tradition of Christian Platonism, that in so far as these myths contain truth, it cannot be different from Truth itself; and he therefore uses this mythology to give both density and precision to the true story he is telling. In doing so he enriches his central myth, not of course in a way that

[1] See e.g., Beryl Smalley, *The Bible in the Middle Ages* (1941), pp. 2–3.

sharpens its appeal to the *intelligence*; but that is not the primary purpose of poetry. He is constantly disclaiming these heathen fancies, but as constantly putting them in; in poetry all *buts* are partly *ands*, and an elaborate demonstration of the total difference between *x* and *y* is undertaken only if they are in some occult manner very alike. This is commonly admitted; no passage in *Paradise Lost* is more admired than that in which Milton explains that Proserpina's 'faire field / Of *Enna*' (iv. 268–69) was not Eden; and everybody remembers such references as those to Mulciber, and the fabled Hesperidean fruit. A less famous but very brilliant example of the method is in Raphael's greeting of Eve in Book V:

but *Eve*
Undeckt, save with her self more lovely fair
Than Wood-Nymph, or the fairest Goddess feignd
Of three that in Mount *Ida* naked strove,
Stood to entertain her guest from Heav'n; no veile
Shee needed, Vertue-proof, no thought infirme
Alterd her cheek. On whom the Angel *Haile*
Bestowd, the holy salutation us'd
Long after to blest *Marie*, second *Eve*.

(v. 379–87)

The first thing we notice is the 'feignd', which puts this myth of the Judgement of Paris in its place. Allegorically the Judgement was normally used to illustrate the disastrousness of a young man's choosing the voluptuous rather than the active or contemplative way of life; but Milton, by emphasizing the difference between Venus and Eve, is able to dispense with such excuses for paganism. Paris, not Venus, entertained guests from heaven, and he was not virtue-proof. But the real point is to associate Eve with both Venus and the Virgin: first the charged negative comparison with the goddess, then the *Ave* proper to Mary. As Mary is the second Eve, so is Eve the second Aphrodite, with all her contradictory attributes: her beauty is perpetually renewed, as Milton himself says in the fifth Latin elegy (I. 103); she is the patroness of fertility; she is dedicated under one aspect to order, and under another to voluptuous disorder and temptation. Under both characters she presides over the Garden of Love.[1] It is impossible

[1] See e.g., E. G. Kern, 'The Gardens of the Decameron Cornice', *Publication of the Modern Language Association of America*, xvi (1951), 505–23.

that plain discourse should say so much about the Eve of the poem as this Venus-Eve-Mary triad suggests, especially if one remembers how wonderfully it is augmented by Adam's chastened echo of it after the Fall:

> the bitterness of death
> Is past, and we shall live. Whence Haile to thee,
> *Eve* rightly calld, Mother of all Mankind.
> (xi. 157–9)

Here is Mary's *Ave*; but here too the *Venus genetrix* of Lucretius: *per te quoniam omne animantum concipitur*. This is Milton's way of exploiting the sensuous illogic by which poetry makes its unparaphrasable points.

Milton, one may safely suggest, was no more naïve about his naïve subject than we are. If the style of the Scriptures is plain and perspicuous, his is not. If they assume that we can best understand the truth in a chronological arrangement, he does not. If they contain all things necessary to salvation, his poem contains both less and more, including a good deal that Milton doubtless believed to be true, but also a good deal that he did not. He sophisticates—or, with Schiller's sense in mind, 'sentimentalizes' might be better—his naïve subject; he is writing for the corrupt and intelligent. The original story, of inexhaustibly various significance for every individual, was there and known; and it would be absurd to suppose that Milton believed himself, in treating it, to be in full control of its affective power, no matter how much he might assume the right of the epic poet to intervene —to comment, to point out (Waldock found this distressing), that Adam was here being fondly overcome with female charm, or that Satan was there glozing. The more vitality he gets into the embodiment of the myth, the less adequate these comments will be; nothing he could say *about* Adam at that wonderful moment could seem adequate to the situation realized in the poem—a man's first glimpse of corruption and mortality, life a great symbolic attitude.

All this is by way of opposing the notion that Milton's known views on scriptural inerrancy need prevent his myth working as it ought in a poem. His invention was not restrained by it; if he could not think with *his* story he could perfectly well think with *this* story. And his freedom to do so may be asserted yet more convincingly by a moment's consideration for what Milton thought to be the province of poetry—what he thought poems were for.

The Province of Poetry

To start from an obvious point: why does he not grind his formidable array of theological axes in the poem? For he certainly does not. The answer cannot be that he considered doing so and then rejected the notion as indecorous, nor that, as Rajan thinks,[1] he put heresies into the poem only in veiled and oblique passages. In fact, it would not have occurred to Milton that poetry was a suitable medium for theological dispute. By an exercise of tact which, whether successful or not, is bold, he sets out the theological rules of the poem in Book iii as coming straight from God himself; there should be no room for argument so far as the poem is concerned about something very difficult and controverted which, though not at the heart of the work, had yet to be in it. He rather drily plots the whole course of human history according to the official point of view, and does it before we have even encountered Adam and Eve. This boldness is characteristic, and can also be seen at points where Milton does happen to think his own views relevant to the poem; there he puts them in, when many think he would have done well to leave them out, as for instance in his insistence on the materiality of angels. The reason is clear: this belief, like his mortalism and his rejection of creation *ex nihilo*, is related to his feelings about life in general. Thus, if he was to have angels, he could afford to be pretty free with angelic lore in general (R. H. West has shown that Milton includes what he did not literally believe)[2] but not to hint at any discontinuity between body and spirit. This was more important to Milton than any other single belief, and he makes Raphael read a lecture on it (v. 469 ff.); it helped him to find the human situation tolerable and it infringed nothing in Scripture, so the angels eat and make love. He is risking a lot here, but not to make a theological or philosophical point. Milton wrote a theological treatise; but *Paradise Lost* is not it.

[1] *Paradise Lost and the Seventeenth Century Reader* (1947), Cap. II, and especially p. 35.

[2] *Milton and the Angels* (1955), p. 101.

It could not have occurred to him to make it so; he would have thought a mere commonplace Cowley's remark that 'if any man design to compose a *Sacred Poem*, only by turning a story of the Scripture, like Mr. *Quarles's*, or some other godly matter, like Mr. *Heywood of Angels,* into *Rhyme*; he is so far from elevating of *Poesie* that he only *abases Divinity*'.[1] From all Milton says about the way poetry works it is clear that he asks of it not that it should *immediately* instruct, but that it should immediately delight; and he presumably accepted some approximation of the Thomist gradations of logical discourse, which run from syllogistic certitude through dialectic, rhetorical probability and sophistic, down to poetry, which offers 'no better than a plausible estimate of the truth'.[2] Even in Hell, the song which suspends Hell and ravishes the audience is less sweet and elevated than the discourse, though fallacious, of the angels who 'reason'd high / Of Providence'; for, as Milton explains parenthetically, 'Eloquence the Soul, Song charms the Sense' (ii. 552–9).

Indeed, we shall always be standing at the wrong angle to *Paradise Lost* if we do not understand what Milton meant by his most celebrated critical observation, the remark that poetry is 'subsequent, or indeed rather precedent to logic' because it is 'less subtle and fine, but more simple, sensuous and passionate' (*Tractate of Education*). By 'simple' I take it Milton means what Fracastoro had in mind when he described poetry as the art *simpliciter bene dicendi*, of speaking well without other end; for the poet as a poet . . . does not develop the matter enough to explain it . . . all the others speak well and appropriately but not simply'.[3] The poet is concerned to transmit not explanations but delight, though there may be much benefit in this appeal to the senses, since poetry has the power 'to allay the perturbations of the mind, and set the affections in right tune' (*The Reason of Church-Government*). The fundamental point is that poetry works through the senses; admittedly *dati sunt sensus ad intellectum excitandum*, but this is a more devious and uncertain route to the

[1] Preface to *Poems* (1656).

[2] W. J. Ong, 'The Province of Rhetoric and Poetic', *Modern Schoolman*, xix (1942), 25, quoting Aquinas; cited in W. K. Wimsatt, *The Verbal Icon* (1954), p. 223.

[3] Quoted in Madeline Doran, *Endeavours of Art* (1954), p. 28. See also pp. 87 ff.

mind than logic and the other kinds of discourse. It is therefore entirely consistent, though still a little surprising, that Milton could say this: 'the words of a Psalm are too full of poetry, and this Psalm too full of passion, to afford us any exact definitions of right and justice; nor is it proper to argue anything of that nature from them' (*The Tenure of Kings and Magistrates*). Now for Milton the Psalms were the highest and most truthful of all poetry, 'to all true tasts excelling' (*Paradise Regained*, iv. 347); and he would apply this stricture, *a fortiori*, to *Paradise Lost*. He would, then, presumably deplore the amount of attention paid to its definitions of right and justice at the expense of its passion and poetry.

Poetry, since it works upon the passions, can obviously be dangerous if dishonestly directed or interpreted; and Milton speaks of the dangers to youth in libidinous poetasters and his own tactful handling of unchaste elegiac poets (*Smectymnuus*). He took the traditional view that a poet ought to be a good man, but he also thought that readers should be trained in virtue; his educational scheme allows the young men to study poetry only after they have been through the curriculum, and after they have reached the stage of *Proairesis*, that act of reason which enables them to contemplate upon moral good and evil. In short, he regards poetry, because of its predominantly sensuous nature, its working through the passions, as a force not of its nature entirely within the control of the author; the hearer's passions are under the control of his own reason, if of anybody's, and he can turn poetry to ill or to good. Milton would doubtless have considered those readers who heroise Satan to be either corrupt or imperfectly educated; but I do not think he would have argued that there was not, in some sense, an heroic Satan *in* the poem. To say that poetry appeals to the mind through the senses, and this is central to Milton's view of the function of poetry, is to admit that the poet's work can never be exactly regulated by his moral intention.

Nor is this doctrine isolated from Milton's more general ideas. As we shall see, his world, as *Paradise Lost* presents it, is unintelligible unless one gives due place to his remarkable insistence on the human capacity for pleasure—delight—and the relation of this to Man's possession of an immortal soul. The poem is primarily about the pleasures of Adam and their destruction by death; about the contrast between a world we can imagine, in which the senses are constantly and innocently enchanted, and a world of which this is not true. This is a contrast with which I shall be much occupied. It is responsible obviously, for much sophistication of the naïve material, and that in a manner very different from the theologian's or the philosopher's. It could not be presented in any other mode of discourse, and required the constant exercise of devices that may be called counterlogical. That *Paradise Lost* is in some sense counterlogical in presentation may strike anyone who has read the logical treatment of the Genesis passages in *De Doctrina* as self-evident; but it is worth mentioning because it is rarely mentioned. Milton in the poem is not aiming directly at the truth, but at the perturbed senses by means of delight; the planning of this circuitous route to the mind of the reader is an elaborate exercise in counterlogic.

Counterlogical Elements

The syntax of the poem is a powerful counterlogical agent. I notice that Dr. Davie decides that the dislocation of normal word-order works well in some places and not in others; and his demonstration is convincing. But he concludes that the practice itself betokens a failure to give proper value to a forward-moving narrative; when in truth movement in time is almost irrelevant to Milton's purpose. The syntax of the poem enables the texture of it to reflect the forces that govern its structure, the great contrasts which have nothing to do with chronological time because they are in the human condition as an inextricable pattern of dark and light, joy and woe, order and chaos, life and death, all making sense as a Latin sentence does, and also using the '. . . and then' as simply another form of emphasis.

One of the undoubted rediscoveries of the Renaissance was 'an awareness of syntactical process;[1] and only recently Professor F. T. Prince, in what is probably the most important book to have been written about Milton since the war, has made it plain that this rediscovery had a direct impact upon poetry. Milton's dislocations derive historically from Bembo's insistence on the latinization of the vulgar, so far as the vulgar could support this, as a means to gravity and pleasure; and Milton alone 'realized

[1] R. G. Faithfull, review of P. A. Verburg, *Taal en Functionaliteit,* in *Archivum Linguisticum,* vii (1953), 146.

the dream of Tasso and his predecessors'[1] by carrying to the necessary degree of 'magnificence' both the distortion of vulgar word-order and *asprezza* of diction and prosody—that disconnected speaking, *parlar disgiunto*, those tricks of elision and consonantal accumulation—thought proper to a topic seminally grave and pleasant. In treating his topic, the simple myth, in a manner so clearly conscious of the historical development of human speech, Milton betrays the counterlogical complexity of his aim; for some purposes, not those of poetry, such complexity might be wickedness, but here it draws attention to the whole human experience under consideration. For in the fallen world pleasure is complex, and demands, as the price of its presence, that all routes to the reason be made difficult. The necessary deformation of language, which is both grave and pleasant, reflects the deformation of the faculty by which Adam named the beasts and Eve the flowers; it shows, though with delight, the difficulties under which we labour to repair the ruins of our first parents.

The most potent of counterlogical devices in verse is rhyme; and it may be asked why Milton, if bent on counterlogic, so unambiguously spurned it. Rhyme was, of course, inconsistent with the intention to achieve *latinità in volgare*; and in his note on the verse Milton calls rhyme 'no necessary Adjunct' of heroic verse, and labels it 'the Invention of a barbarous Age'; already it had been discarded by Italian and Spanish poets 'of prime note' as 'trivial and of no true musical delight; which consists only in apt Numbers, fit quantity of Syllables, and the sense variously drawn out from one Verse into another, not in the jingling sound of like endings'. To get rid of rhyme is to restore 'ancient liberty'.

Rhyme as a mark of bondage and inferiority is a notion likely enough to crop up in a post-Renaissance literature; yet even while its Gothic character was recognized, the possibilities it offered for counterlogical effects were most fully exploited. The special effects to be had from the collocation of ideas which, apparently totally heterogeneous, are momentarily exhibited, by the agency of rhyme, as possessing a magical resemblance, have been studied in Mr. W. K. Wimsatt's brilliant essay on Pope's rhymes.[2] Full

[1] *The Italian Element in Milton's Verse* (1954), p. 13.

[2] 'Rhetoric and Poems: Alexander Pope', in *English Institute Essays* 1948 (1949); reprinted in *The Verbal Icon* (1953).

rhyming (though the fullest, *rime riche*, was not licensed in England) is absolutely and intrusively illogical. Dr. Johnson thought rhyme should be intrusive, and disliked the remoteness of the rhymes in poems by Milton and Gray; and it may be that the rhyme of the *canzone*, which Milton imitates, is proper only to a language in which rhyme, because it is easier, is required to make less impact that it normally does in English. Later on there is great variety of rhyme in English—it is varied with half-rhyme, it is muted in different ways, it is employed internally and almost undetectably; but this comes in with poetry which is in other ways so clearly distinguished from logical discourse that there is no need to insist on its illogic. Milton might have found rhyme useful; but he had the failure of Cowley's biblical epic to warn him off, and he had all the resources of dislocated word order, of *parlar disgiunto*, in its place.

Nevertheless, there is more rhyming in *Paradise Lost* than people think,[1] and there is also a great deal of what may be called 'pseudo-rhyme'. It serves with all the other devices to distance logic. Milton, as F. T. Prince has shown, learned something of 'submerged rhyme' from the Italian Rota;[2] and, though I was writing out of the ignorance that prevailed before the publication of Prince's book, I still think there may be something in an old guess of my own that Milton was interested in a pretty widely held theory that the Psalms used rhyme and half-rhyme. Sometimes the rhymes in *Paradise Lost* may seem accidental:

> Thither let us *tend*,
> From off the tossing of these fiery waves,
> There rest, if any rest can harbour *there*,
> And reassembling our afflicted Powers,
> Consult how we may henceforth most *offend*
> Our Enemy, our own loss how *repair*,
> How overcome this dire Calamity,
> What reinforcement we may gain from Hope,
> If not what resolution from *despair*.
>
> (i. 183–91)

[1] See an elaborate study of the rhymes by J. S. Diekhoff, *P.M.L.A.*, xlix (1934).

[2] *op. cit.*, pp. 78–81.

I have here marked the full rhymes, but they only reinforce the other conjunctions of opposites, such as the very characteristic 'hope-despair' of the last two lines quoted. This kind of antithesis, especially when strengthened by the placing of each term at the end of a line, is a kind of pseudo-rhyming that goes on throughout the poem. I open the work at Book v and find *all/all* (470–1), *will/fate* (526–7), the short story of *will/fall/fall'n/fall/woe*! (539–43), and the strong thematic triad *free/love/command* (549–51). In the superb passage where Satan, having, 'stupidly good', contemplated the beauty of Eve, bends himself to the task of corrupting it, there is this fit of elaborate internal pseudo-rhyming, brought to a close with a terminal half-rhyme.

> Shee fair, divinely fair, fit Love for Gods,
> Not terrible, though terror be in Love
> And beautie, not approacht by stronger hate,
> Hate stronger, under shew of Love well feignd,
> The way which to her ruin now I tend.
>
> (ix. 489–93)

And this whole passage echoes the lines describing Satan's first sight of Eve, where there is this play with *delight*, *joy*, *woe* and *foe*:

> Ah gentle pair, ye little think how nigh
> Your change approaches, when all these delights
> Will vanish and deliver ye to woe,
> More woe, the more your taste is now of joy;
> Happie, but for so happie ill secur'd
> Long to continue, and this high seat your Heav'n
> Ill fenc't for Heav'n to keep out such a foe
> As now is enterd . . .
>
> (iv. 366–73)

The force of this comes generally from the conviction with which the human predicament is stated ('for so happie ill secur'd') but the impact depends upon the placing of 'woe' and 'foe', 'delights' and 'joy', and also of 'nigh' and 'Ill'. There are a dozen other ways, rhetorical devices common and uncommon, of getting the effect of surprising rhyme without recourse to barbarous jingle: for instance, 'O fair foundation laid whereon to build /

Thir ruin!' (iv. 521–2). This is, in the first place, a cruel paradox; one doesn't, or at this date didn't, build ruins. But there is also a pun-like effect using two senses of *ruin*, not only what is left after the destructive act, but also the fall itself—a sense which was still primary at the date of *Paradise Lost*. Another kind of pseudo-rhyming is found in some of Satan's close and fallacious argument, which not only gives the impression of being very tightly bound by phonetic repetitions but works like magic in deceiving Eve; consider, for instance, the brilliant lines ix. 694–702. If anybody doubts the truth of Richardson's well-known remark that the reader of Milton needs to be continually on duty, let him re-read this passage and ask himself if he has always understood the argument by which Satan reaches his conclusion, 'Your feare it self of Death removes the fear' (702). His methods are rhetorical, but he is not interested in truth; this is a special kind of incantation aimed at the sense. One magic expression, 'death denounc't' continues hereafter to echo irrationally from this book of the Fall, through the next book, which is of despair: ix. 695, x. 49, 210, 852–3, 962.

It seems, then, that Milton did not abjure rhyme as an impediment to his dealing directly with the doctrinal substance of the theme, but because he had more complicated uses for it, more refined ideas about the way to achieve musical delight; his counterlogic is a vastly more subtle affair than a mere tagging of verses. And musical delight, before instruction, is his aim.[1].

We may conclude that there is reason to suppose that we shall miss the force of Milton's poem if we assume that he was strictly limited by the *naïveté* of his theme or the inerrancy of its biblical expression. His method is to affect the senses of his audience and not its reason directly. He could not have hoped for total control over the affective power of the poem, for that is not consistent with the nature of poetry; and in this particular poem the material is common property, so that there must be many aspects of it which interest other people and not Milton, yet cannot be excluded. The original myth is a myth of total explanation, and

[1] Here the reader might find it useful to be reminded of a remarkable passage on the rhetoric of irregular rhyming in Allen Tate's commentary on his own *Ode to the Confederate Dead,* 'Narcissus as Narcissus', *Reason in Madness*, 1935.

therefore infinitely explicable; the poet can only say some of the things about it but the rest of it is still in men's minds, or indeed below them—Joyce's umbilical telephone line to Edenville. It is not of course doubted that Milton does offer interpretations, that he gets at the reader in many ways; the theology of Book iii, for example, is made to sound very dogmatic, though only to prevent irrelevant speculation; and we are always being told the proper way to think about Satan. As well as presenting the human predicament the poet suggests ways of understanding and accepting it. It should even be admitted that the general design of the poem is governed by this double purpose of presentation and interpretation; and that not only in the strategic theologizing of the third book and the loaded education of Adam between Books iv and ix. For although it is commonly said that Milton, on the ancient epic pattern, proceeds *in medias res*, he in fact strikes into his subject nothing like so near the middle as Virgil and Homer; he starts not in the Garden but with the fall of the angels, which is why some schoolchildren, having read Books i and ii, go through life thinking it was Satan who lost paradise. The reason for this, one guesses, is that Milton wanted us to think of events in this order: the Fall from heaven, the Fall from Paradise, and finally the effect of the Fall in the life of humanity in general, just in the manner of Ignatian meditation on these subjects.[1] But it is important that we should not allow considerations of this sort to lead to a conviction that there is at all times a design upon us. So deceived, we can easily miss something far more obvious and important to the structure of the poem: namely, that it is based on a series of massive antitheses, or if you like huge structural pseudo-rhymes, and the central pseudo-rhyme is *delight/woe*. The delight and woe are here and now, which is the real point of all the squeezing together of the time-sequence that Milton carries on in his similes, in upsetting allusions to clerical corruption, in using expressions like 'never since created man' or 'since mute'; in a hundred other ways, some of which I shall discuss later. The poem is absolutely contemporary, and its subject is human experience symbolized in this basic myth, and here made relevant in a manner not so different from that to which our own century has accustomed us.

[1] See for example *The Sermons and Devotional Writings of Gerard Manly Hopkins*, ed. C. Devlin (1959), pp. 131 ff.

The Themes

Miss Rosemond Tuve, in her magnificent and too brief book, has persuasively expounded Milton's treatment in the minor poems of certain great central themes. They lie at the heart of each poem and govern its secondary characteristics of imagery and diction; given the theme, the poet thinks in the figures appropriate to it, and in every case the theme and the figures have a long and rich history. 'The subject of *L'Allegro* is every man's Mirth, our Mirth, the very Grace herself with all she can include';[1] the *Hymn on the Morning of Christ's Nativity* proliferates images of harmony because its theme is the Incarnation. I now take a step of which Miss Tuve would probably not approve, and add that beneath these figures and themes there is Milton's profound and personal devotion to an even more radical topic, potentially coextensive with all human experience: the loss of Eden. In the *Hymn* there is a moment of peace and harmony in history—the 'Augustan peace', which looks back to human wholeness and incorruption, as well as forward to a time when, after generations of human anguish, the original harmony will be restored. The same moment of stillness, poised between past and future, is there in 'At a Solemn Musick', for music remembers as well as prefigures. In *Comus* too there is presented that moment of harmony, of reunion and restitution, that prefigures the final end, and in *Comus* as in the others there is an emphasis on the long continuance of grief and suffering; for in the much misunderstood Epilogue Adonis is still not cured of his wound and Venus 'sadly sits'. Only in the future will Cupid be united with Psyche and the twins of Paradise, Youth and Joy, be born. *Lycidas* tells of disorder, corruption, false glory as incident to life here and now, with order, health, and the perfect witness of God to come. All of them speak of something that is gone.

Paradise Lost deals most directly with this basic theme, the recognition of lost possibilities of joy, order, health, the contrast between what we can imagine as human and what is so here and now; the sensuous import of the myth of the lost Eden. To embody this theme is the main business of *Paradise Lost*; thus will life be displayed in some great symbolic attitude and not by the poet's explanations of the how and the why. His first task is to get clear the human experience of the potency of delight, and its

[1] *Images and Themes in Five Poems by Milton* (1957), p. 20.

necessary frustration, and if he cannot do that the poem will fail no matter what is added of morality, theology or history.

My difficulty in establishing this point is that some will think it too obvious to be thus laboured, and others will think it in need of much more elaborate defence. What is rare is to find people who read *Paradise Lost* as if it were true that the power of joy and its loss is its theme; and though it is true that for certain well-known and important reasons Milton's poem is not accessible to the same methods of reading as Romantic literature, it is also true that this is the theme of *The Prelude*, and that we can do some harm by insisting too strongly upon differences at the expense of profound similarities. Anyway, I think I can make my point in a somewhat different way by a reference to Bentley, and in particular to his observations on the last lines of *Paradise Lost*, stale as this subject may seem.

Adam, hearing Michael's promise of a time when 'Earth / Shall all be Paradise, far happier place / Than this of *Eden*' (xii. 463–5) is 'replete with joy and wonder' (468) and replies with the famous cry of *felix culpa*:

> full of doubt I stand,
> Whether I should repent me now of sin
> By mee done and occasiond, or rejoice
> Much more, that much more good thereof shall spring . . .
> (473–6)

Michael says that the Comforter will watch over and arm the faithful; Adam, benefiting by Michael's foretelling of the future (in which 'time stands fixt' as it does in the poem) has now all possible wisdom (575–6); and Eve is well content with her lot. And thus matters stand when Eden is closed, and Adam and Eve move away

> The World was all before them, where to choose
> Thir place of rest, and Providence thir guide:
> They hand in hand with wandring steps and slow,
> Through *Eden* took thir solitarie way.
> (xii. 646–9)

'Why' asks Bentley, 'does this distich dismiss our first parents in anguish, and the reader in melancholy? And how can the expression be justified, *with wandring steps and slow*? Why *wandring*?

Erratick steps? Very improper, when, in the line before, they were *guided by Providence*. And why slow? even when Eve has professed her readiness and alacrity for the journey:

> but now lead on;
> In me is no delay.

And why their *solitarie way*? All words to represent a sorrowful parting? when even their former walks in Paradise were as solitary as their way now; there being nobody besides them two both here and there. Shall I therefore, after so many prior presumptions, presume at last to offer a distich, as close as may be to the author's words, and *entirely agreeable to his scheme*?

> Then hand in hand with *social* steps their way
> Through Eden took, *with heavenly comfort cheer'd*.'

Bentley assumes that he has exact knowledge of Milton's 'scheme', and quarrels with the text for not fitting it. He seems to be forgetting God's instructions to Michael—'so send them forth, though sorrowing, yet in peace' (xi. 117), and also Adam's knowledge of the events leading up to the happy consummation; yet it remains true that if Milton's 'scheme' was simply to show that everything would come out right in the end, and that this should keenly please both Adam and ourselves, Bentley is not at all silly here; or if he is, so are more modern commentators who, supported by all that is now known about the topic *felix culpa*, tend to read the poem in a rather similar way though without actually rewriting it, by concentrating on Milton's intention, somewhat neglected in the past, to present this belated joy of Adam's as central to the whole poem. There is, of course, such an intention or 'scheme'; the mistake is to suppose that it is paramount. It is in fact subsidiary, *Paradise Lost* being a poem, to the less explicable theme of joy and woe, which has to be expressed in terms of the myth, as a contrast between the original justice of Paradise and the mess of history: between Paradise and Paradise lost. The poem is tragic. If we regard it as a document in the history of ideas, ignoring what it does to our senses, we shall of course find ideas, as Bentley did, and conceivably the closing lines will seem out of true. But our disrespect for Bentley's Milton, and in this place particularly, is proof that the poem itself will prevent our doing this unless we are very stubborn or not very susceptible to poetry. The last lines of the poem are, we *feel*, exactly right, for all that Adam has cried out for pleasure; death denounced, he has lost his Original Joy. The tragedy is a matter of *fact*, of life as we feel it; the hope of restoration is a matter of faith, and faith is 'the substance of things hoped for, the evidence of things unseen'—a matter altogether less simple, sensuous, and passionate, altogether less primitive. We are reminded that 'the conception that man is mortal, by his nature and essence, seems to be entirely alien to mythical and primitive religious thought'.[1] In the poem we deplore the accidental loss of native immortality more than we can applaud its gracious restoration.

Adam Imparadised

One of the effects of mixing up Milton with the Authorized Version, and of intruding mistaken ideas of Puritanism into his verse, is that it can become very hard to see what is made absolutely plain: that for Milton the joy of Paradise is very much a matter of the senses. The Authorized Version says that 'the Lord God planted a garden' (Gen. ii. 8) and that he 'took the man and put him into the garden of Eden to dress it and keep it' (ii. 15). But even in Gen. ii. 8 the Latin texts usually have *in paradisum voluptatis* 'into a paradise of pleasure'—this is the reading of the Vulgate currently in use. And the Latin version of ii. 15 gives *in paradiso deliciarum*. Milton's Paradise is that of the Latin version; in it, humanity without guilt is 'to all delight of human sense expos'd' (iv. 206), and he insists on this throughout. Studying the exegetical tradition on this point, Sister Mary Corcoran makes it plain that Milton pushes this sensuous pleasure much harder than his 'scheme' as Bentley and others might conceive it, required. For example, he rejected the strong tradition that the first marriage was not consummated until after the Fall, choosing to ignore the difficulty about children conceived before but born after it. For this there may be an historical explanation in the Puritan cult of married love; but it could not account for what has been called Milton's 'almost Dionysiac treatment'[2] of sexuality before the Fall; Sister Corcoran is sorry that she can't even

[1] E. Cassirer, *An Essay on Man* (1944), pp. 83–4.

[2] Harris Fletcher, *Milton's Rabbinical Readings* (1930), p. 185.

quite believe the assertion that 'in those hearts / Love unlibidinous reignd (v. 449–50).[1]

In fact Milton went to great trouble to get this point firmly made; had he failed no amount of finesse in other places could have held the poem together; and it is therefore just as well that nothing in the poem is more beautifully achieved.

Why was innocent sexuality so important to Milton's poem? Why did he take on the task of presenting an Adam and an Eve unimaginably privileged in the matter of sensual gratification 'to all delight of human sense expos'd'? There is a hint of the answer in what I have written earlier about his view of the function of poetry. Believing as he did in the inseparability of matter and form, except by an act of intellectual abstraction, Milton could not allow a difference of kind between soul and body; God

created all
Such to perfection, one first matter all,
Indu'd with various forms, various degrees
Of substance, and in things that live, of life;
But more refin'd, more spiritous and pure,
As nearer to him plac't or nearer tending
Each in thir several active Sphears assignd,
Till body up to spirit work, in bounds
Proportiond to each kind. So from the root
Springs lighter the green stalk, from thence the leaves
More aerie, last the bright consummat flowre
Spirits odorous breathes: flowrs and thir fruit
Mans nourishment, by gradual scale sublim'd
To vital Spirits aspire, to animal,
To intellectual, give both life and sense,
Fancie and understanding, whence the Soule
Reason receives, and reason is her being,
Discursive or Intuitive; discourse
Is oftest yours, the latter most is ours . . .
(v. 471–89)

An acceptance of Raphael's position involves, given the cosmic scale of the poem, a number of corollaries which Milton does not shirk. Matter, the medium of the senses, is continuous with spirit; or 'spirit, being the more excellent substance, virtually and

[1] *Paradise Lost with reference to the Hexameral Background* (1945), pp. 76 ff.

essentially contains within itself the inferior one; as the spiritual and rational faculty contains the corporeal, that is, the sentient and vegetative faculty' (*De Doctrina Christiana* I. vii). It follows that the first matter is of God, and contains the potentiality of form;[1] so the body is not to be thought of in disjunction from the soul, of which 'rational', 'sensitive' and 'vegetative' are merely aspects. Raphael accordingly goes out of his way to explain that the intuitive reason of the angels differs only in degree from the discursive reason of men; and Milton that there is materiality in angelic spirit. It is a consequence of this that part of Satan's sufferings lie in a deprivation of sensual pleasure. Milton's thought is penetrated by this doctrine, which, among other things, accounts for his view of the potency of poetry for good or ill; for poetry works through pleasure, by sensuous delight; it can help 'body up to spirit work' or it can create dangerous physiological disturbance. Obviously there could be no more extreme challenge to the power and virtue of his art than this: to require of it a representation of ecstatic sensual pleasure, a *voluptas* here and only here not associated with the possibility of evil: 'delight to Reason join'd' (ix. 243). The loves of Paradise must be an unimaginable joy to the senses, yet remain 'unlibidinous'.

If we were speaking of Milton rather than of his poem we might use this emphasis on materiality, on the dignity as well as the danger of sense, to support a conclusion similar to that of De Quincey in his account of Wordsworth: 'his intellectual passions were fervent and strong; but they rested upon a basis of preternatural animal sensibility diffused through *all* the animal passions (or appetites); and something of that will be found to hold of all poets who have been great by original force and power...' (De Quincey was thinking about Wordsworth's facial resemblance to Milton). And it would be consistent with such an account that Milton also had, like Wordsworth, a constant awareness of the dangers entailed by a powerful sensibility. This gives us the short reason why, when Milton is representing the enormous bliss of innocent sense, he does not do so by isolating it and presenting it straightforwardly. He sees that we must grasp it at best deviously; we understand joy as men partially deprived of it, with a strong sense of the woeful gap between the possible

[1] See W. B. Hunter, Jr., 'Milton's Power of Matter', *Journal of the History of Ideas,* xiii (1952), 551–62.

and the actual in physical pleasure. And Milton's prime device for ensuring that we should thus experience his Eden is a very sophisticated, perhaps a 'novelistic' one: we see all delight through the eyes of Satan.

Points of View

I shall return to this, and to the other more or less distorting glasses that Milton inserts between us and the voluptuousness of Eden; but first it seems right to say a word in general on a neglected subject, Milton's varying of the point of view in this poem. He uses the epic poet's privilege of intervening in his own voice, and he does this to regulate the reader's reaction; but some of the effects he gets from this device are far more complicated than is sometimes supposed. The corrective comments inserted after Satan has been making out a good case for himself are not to be lightly attributed to a crude didacticism; naturally they are meant to keep the reader on the right track, but they also allow Milton to preserve the energy of the myth. While we are hearing Satan we are not hearing the comment; for the benefit of a fallen audience the moral correction is then applied, but its force is calculatedly lower; and the long-established custom of claiming that one understands Satan better than Milton did is strong testimony to the tact with which it is done. On this method the devil can have good tunes. Not only does his terrible appearance resemble an eclipse which 'with fear of change / Perplexes Monarchs' (i. 598–9), but his oratory can include sound republican arguments—God is 'upheld by old repute, / Consent or custom' (639–40). This sort of thing makes its point before the authorial intervention corrects it. Milton even takes the risk of refraining from constant intervention and Satan-baiting in the first book, where the need for magnificence and energy is greatest. It is the second that the intense persuasions of the angelic debaters are firmly qualified; the speech of Belial is a notable case, for it is poignantly and humanly reasonable, but hedged before and behind by sharp comments on its hollowness and lack of nobility. We may find this argument attractive, but we ought to know that it has a wider moral context, and this the comment provides. At the other extreme, when God is laying down the law or Raphael telling Adam what he needs to know, the presentation is bare and unambiguous not because there is nothing the author wants to draw one's attention to but because these are not the places to start on the difficult question of how the reader's senses enhance or distort the truth; it is when the fallen study the deviousness of the fallen that corrective comment is called for, but even there sense must be given its due.

Of all the feats of narrative sophistication in the poem the most impressive is the presentation of the delights of Paradise under the shadow of Satan. He approaches out of chaos and darkness; a warning voice cries 'Woe to th'inhabitants on Earth' (iv. 5); he is 'inflam'd with rage' (9) as he moves in on calm and joy; and the consequences of the coming encounter are prefigured in the terminal words of lines 10–12: *Mankind . . . loss . . . Hell.* Before him Eden lies 'pleasant' (28); but we are not to see the well-tempered joys of its inhabitants before we have studied, with Uriel in the sun, the passionate fact of Satan, marred by 'distempers foule' (118), a condition possible only to the fallen. He fares forward to Eden, 'delicious Paradise' (132); distemper and delight are about to meet. A good deal is made of the difficulty of access to Eden; not, I think, because Satan would find it difficult—he 'in contempt / At one slight bound high overleap'd all bound' (180–1)—but because *we* must find it so; we are stumbling, disorientated, with Satan into an unintelligible purity:

And of pure now purer aire
Meets his approach, and to the heart inspires
Vernal delight and joy, able to drive
All sadness but despair: now gentle gales
Fanning thir odoriferous wings dispense
Native perfumes, and whisper whence they stole
Those baumie spoils. As when to them who sail
Beyond the *Cape of Hope*, and now are past
Mozambic, off at Sea North-East winds blow
Sabean Odours from the spicie shore
Of *Arabie* the blest, with such delay
Well pleas'd they slack thir course, and many a League
Cheerd with the grateful smell old Ocean smiles.
So entertaind those odorous sweets the Fiend
Who came thir bane, though with them better pleas'd
Than *Asmodeus* with the fishie fume,
That drove him, though enamourd, from the Spouse

> Of *Tobits* Son, and with a vengeance sent
> From *Media* post to *Egypt*, there fast bound.
>
> (152–71)

This passage is preceded by praises of the colours of Paradise, and of delights directed at the senses of hearing, touch and taste; here the sense of smell is predominant, and Milton provides a remarkable association of fallen and unfallen odours. What becomes of the scents of Eden? They decay, and another smell replaces them, as Death himself will describe:

> a scent I draw
> Of carnage, prey innumerable, and taste
> The savour of Death from all things there that live . . .
> So saying, with delight he snuffd the smell
> Of mortal change on Earth.
>
> (x. 267 ff.)

At first Milton uses a lot of force to establish a situation lacking entirely this evil smell. 'Of pure now purer aire'—we are moving into the very centre of purity, delight and joy, where no sadness could survive save irredeemable hopelessness (a hint that even this purity cannot repel Satan). The breezes carry scents which betray their paradisal origin: 'baumie' is a key-word in the life-asserting parts of the poem, being used in the sense in which Donne uses it in the 'Nocturnall', as referring to the whole principle of life and growth; compare 'virtue', meaning natural vitality, in the same parts. The simile of the perfumes drifting out to sea from Arabia Felix refers to this breeze-borne odour, but also, with a characteristic and brilliant syntactical turn, to its effect upon Satan, the next topic treated; 'as when' seems at first to refer back, then to refer forward. This effect is helped by the Miltonic habit of boxing off formal similes with fullstops before and after. Satan checks himself at this influx of sensual delight; but we are reminded, with maximum force, of the difference between Satan and the sailors, by the emphatic 'Who came thir bane'. And this dissonance prepares us for the fuller ambiguities introduced by the reference to Asmodeus, a lustful devil who was driven away from Sarah by the stink of burning fish-liver. Why does Milton go about to fetch Asmodeus into his verses? The point is not the one he explicitly makes, that Satan liked the smell of Eden better than

Asmodeus the smell of fish-liver; anybody who believes that will believe all he is told about Milton's sacrificing sense to sound, and so forth. The point is partly that Satan is also going to be attracted by a woman; partly that he too will end by being, as a direct consequence of his attempt upon her, 'fast bound'; but the poet's principal intention is simply to get into the context a bad smell. The simile offers as an excuse for its existence a perfunctory logical connection with what is being said; but it is used to achieve a purely sensuous effect. As soon as we approach Eden there is a mingling of the good actual odour with a bad one, of Life with Death.

Another rather similar and equally rich effect is produced by another very long sentence, iv. 268–311. From the dance of 'Universal *Pan* / Knit with the *Graces*' (286–7) we pass on to negative comparisons between Eden and other gardens. All the negations work at an unimportant level of discourse; they are denials of similarity which would not be worth making if they did not imply powerful resemblances. Eden is not the vale of Enna, nor Eve Proserpina, nor Satan Dis, nor Ceres Christ. Though Daphne was saved from a devil by a divine act, her grove was not Eden, and though 'old *Cham*' protected in another garden the 'Florid Son' of Amalthea, this does not mean that the garden of Bacchus was the same paradise as that in which another lover of pleasure, almost divine, was, though inadequately, protected. In their unlikeness they all tell us more about the truth of Eden; yet it is upon their unlikeness that Milton is still, apparently, dwelling when his Satan breaks urgently in; they are all

> wide remote
> From this *Assyrian* Garden, where the Fiend
> Saw undelighted all delight. . . .
>
> (285–6)

Whereupon, having included the undelighted Satan in the enormous, delighted scene, Milton goes on, still without a full period, to an elaborate account of Adam and Eve.

The Garden of Love

The degree of literary sophistication in Milton's treatment of the biblical account of Adam and Eve in Paradise is a reasonably accurate index of his whole attitude to what I have called the myth. I have already mentioned the incorporation of other literary and mythological gardens in this Eden; they are significant shadows of it. But the full exploration of the literary context of Milton's Paradise would be a very large inquiry, and here there is occasion only for a brief and tentative sketch of it, touching only upon what affects the present argument.

When Milton comes to treat of the inhabitants of the garden he plunges us at once into a dense literary context. The Bible says: 'And they were both naked, the man and his wife, and were not ashamed' (Genesis ii. 25). According to Milton, however, they were 'with native Honour clad / In naked Majestie' (289–90); and a little later he moralizes this:

> Nor those mysterious parts were then conceal'd,
> Then was not guiltie shame, dishonest shame
> Of Natures works: honor dishonorable,
> Sin-bred, how have ye troubl'd all mankind
> With shews instead, mere shows of seeming pure . . .
> (312–6)

This is in open allusion to a literary topic so often treated in Renaissance and seventeenth-century writing as to be unwieldy in its complexity. First one needs to understand the general primitivistic position which held that custom and honour were shabby modern expedients unnecessary in a Golden Age society, with all its corollaries in Renaissance 'naturalism'. Then one has to consider the extremely complex subject of literary gardens and their connection with the Earthly Paradise and the Golden Age, not only in Renaissance, but also in classical and mediaeval literature. Of the first of these I now say nothing. The easy way to approach the second is through the *locus classicus*, the chorus *O bella étà de l'oro* in Tasso's *Aminta*. In the Golden Age, as in Eden, the earth bore fruit and flowers without the aid of man; the air was calm and there was eternal spring. Best of all, there was continual happiness because—in the translation of Henry Reynolds—

> Because that vain and ydle name,
> That couz'ning Idoll of unrest,
> Whom the madd vulgar first did raize,
> And call'd it Honour, whence it came
> To tyrannize o're ev'ry brest,

Was not then suffred to molest
Poore lovers hearts with new debate. . . .
The Nymphes sate by their Paramours,
Whispring love-sports, and dalliance. . . .

It was Honour that ruined Pleasure,

And lewdly did instruct faire eyes
They should be nyce, and scrupulous . . .
(*Torquato Tassos Aminta Englisht*, 1628)

This is the Honour, a tyrant bred of custom and ignorant opinion, which inevitably intrudes into Milton's argument when he uses the word in forcible oxymoron, 'honor dishonorable'. But he is not using the idea as it came sometimes to be used in poetry Milton would have called dishonest; his Honour is 'sin-bred', a pathetic subterfuge of the fallen, and not, as it is in libertine poems, an obstacle to sexual conquest that must yield to primitivist argument.[1] Of these ambiguities Milton must have been fully aware, since the poetry of his time contains many libertine attacks on Honour which imply that reason and 'native Honour' will be satisfied only by an absolute surrender to pleasure. Furthermore, many of these poems are set in gardens, and we should not overlook the difficulties Milton had to overcome before he could be reasonably satisfied that his garden of love was the right kind. The garden of love has a long history, and the topic nowadays called the *locus amoenus*[2] is as old as the garden of Alcinous in the *Odyssey*; the expression *locus amoenus* meant to Servius 'a place for lovemaking', and *amoenus* was derived by a false etymology from *amor*. This tradition, mingling with the continuous traditions of the Earthly Paradise, and modified by the allegorical skills of the Middle Ages, sometimes conformed and sometimes conflicted with the garden of Genesis; gardens could be the setting for all kinds of love, just as Venus herself could preside over all kinds of love and all kinds of gardens. Milton needed a *paradisus voluptatis*,

[1] I have said part of my say about this in 'The Argument of Marvell's *Garden*', *Essays in Criticism,* ii (1952), 225–241.

[2] See E. R. Curtius, *European Literature in the Latin Middle Ages* (1952), Cap. 10, especially pp. 195 ff. And among the growing literature on this theme, E. G. Kern's article cited in note 1, p. 89.

but it must not be the same as a 'naturalist' or libertine garden, and it must not be connected with 'courtly love'—hence the disclaimers in II. 744 ff. and II. 769–70. Whatever the dishonest and sophisticate, or for that matter the falsely philosophical, might do with imaginary Edens, he was dealing with the thing itself, and must get innocent delight into it. So he uses these conventions, including the usual attack upon Honour, with his customary boldness, as if his treatment, though late, were the central one, and all the others mere shadows of his truth; the same method, in fact, as that used for pagan mythology. In Book ix, having risked all the difficulties of his contrast between love unlibidinous and love libidinous by showing them both in the experience of Adam and Eve, he is able to enlarge upon the oxymoron 'honor dishonorable', saying that

> innocence, that as a veil
> Had shaddowd them from knowing ill, was gon,
> Just confidence and native righteousness,
> And honour from about them. . . .
>
> (ix. 1054–7)

And Adam sees that the fruit of knowledge was bad, 'if this be to know, / Which leaves us naked thus, of Honour void' (1073–4); here the fig-leaves are assimilated to the literary tradition. As for *locus amoenus*, Milton also contrives to give two versions of it: in Book iv it is worked into the account of 'unreprov'd' love-making (see especially II. 1034 ff.) as the scene of the first fallen act of love. Pope first saw another link between these two passages, and Douglas Bush has recently written upon this link a brilliant page of commentary:[1] each derives a good deal, and the manner of derivation is ironical, from a single episode in the *Iliad*, the lovemaking of Zeus and Hera in Book xiv.

So, erudite and delicate, yet so characteristic a device might find, among fit audience, someone to value it for itself; but Milton's object was to exploit, with what force all the literature in the world could lend, the contrast between the true delight of love and the fallacious delight which is a mere prelude to woe; between possible and actual human pleasure. And however complex the means, the end is simply to show Adam and Eve as actually enjoying what to us is a mere imagination, and then

[1] *Paradise Lost in our Time* (1948), pp. 105–6.

explain how they lost it, and what was then left. In this sense their simple experience contains the whole of ours, including that which we feel we might but know we cannot have; and in this sense they include us, they are what we are and what we imagine we might be. This inclusiveness is given remarkably concrete demonstration in lines so famous for their unidiomatic English that the reason for the distorted word-order has been overlooked:

> the lovliest pair
> That ever since in loves imbraces met,
> *Adam* the goodliest man of men since born
> His Sons, the fairest of her Daughters *Eve*.
> (iv. 321–4)

The syntax may be Greek, but the sense is English, and inclusiveness could hardly be more completely presented; Adam and Eve here literally include us all. The illogic of the expression serves the same end as the illogic of those mythological parallels inserted only to be denied, or of those continuous reminders that the whole of history 'since created man' is somehow being enacted here and now in the garden. What must never be underestimated is the sheer absorbency of Milton's theme; everything will go into it, and find itself for the first time properly placed, completely explained. Todd has a note on the passage (iv. 458 ff.) in which Milton adapts to the awakening of Eve Ovid's account of Narcissus first seeing himself in the pool: he cites one commentator who enlarges upon Milton's enormous improvement of Ovid's lines, and another who adds that 'we may apply to Milton on this occasion what Aristotle says of Homer, that he taught poets how to lie properly'. Lying properly about everything is a reasonable way of describing the poet's achievement in *Paradise Lost*, if a proper lie is one that includes the *terra incognita* of human desires, actual love and possible purity.

That is why we see Adam and Eve in the garden of love not directly, but through many glasses; and the darkest of these is the mind of Satan. He looks at his victims with passionate envy and even regret:

> Ah gentle pair, ye little think how nigh
> Your change approaches, when all these delights
> Will vanish and deliver ye to woe,

More woe, the more your taste is now of joy;
Happie, but for so happie ill secur'd
Long to continue, and this high seat your Heav'n
Ill fenc't for Heav'n to keep out such a foe
As now is enterd.

(iv. 366–73)

He is reluctant to harm them; he pleads necessity (Milton calls this 'The Tyrants plea' (394) and neatly gives it to Adam in x. 131 ff.). But what he must take away from them is *delight*, physical pleasure in innocence; his dwelling in Hell 'haply may not please / Like this fair Paradise, your sense' (iv. 378–9). They are to 'taste' something other than Joy; and one remembers how frequently, at critical moments, the word 'taste' occurs in *Paradise Lost*, from the second line on. The shadow of Satan falls most strikingly over the pleasures of the garden when he watches Adam and Eve making love. It is not merely that the absolutely innocent and joyous act is observed as through a peep-hole, as if the lovers had been tricked into a bawdy-house; Satan himself acquires some of the pathos of an old *voyeur*. Pursuing his equation of delight with innocence, Milton boldly hints that the fallen angel is sexually deprived. He has forfeited the unfallen delights of sense. There is, we are to learn, lovemaking in heaven, but not in hell; the price of warring against omnipotence is impotence.

Sight hateful, sight tormenting! thus these two
Imparadis't in one anothers arms
The happier *Eden*, shall enjoy thir fill
Of bliss on bliss, while I to Hell am thrust,
Where neither joy nor love, but fierce desire,
Among our other torments not the least,
Still unfulfilld with pain of longing pines . . .

(iv. 505–11)

Satan is so sure of their sexual joy that he anticipates later love poetry in making the body of the beloved a paradise in itself—his 'happier Eden' is not the same as that promised later to Adam (xii. 587)—and he uses a word, 'imparadis't' which was to have its place in the vocabulary of fallen love. But at this moment only Satan can feel desire without fulfilment, and Milton reminds us that he resembles in this fallen men; thus he actualizes the human contrast between innocence and experience, and between love and its counterfeits—the whole 'monstruosity of love', as Troilus calls it.

Milton, in short, provides an illogical blend of purity and impurity in the first delightful lovemaking. He does not present an isolated purity and then its contamination, as the narrative might seem to require, but interferes with this order just as he does with word-order, and for similar reasons. Not only does he show us the unfallen Adam and Eve in such a way that we can never think of their delight without thinking of its enemies; he also establishes such links between the fourth and ninth books that we can never think of his account of unfallen love without remembering the parallel passages on lust. It is here relevant to emphasize the unpraised brilliance of one of the linking devices, Milton's use of the theme of physiological perturbation. At the opening of Book iv Uriel observes that Satan is affected by unregulated passions, as the unfallen Adam and Eve cannot be; he is the first person on earth to experience this. But by the end of the Book he has established by an act of demonic possession that Eve is physiologically capable of such a disturbance (iv. 799 ff; v. 9–11); and the effect of the Fall in Book ix can be measured by the degree to which the humours of the lovers are distempered by the fruit:

> Soon as the force of that fallacious Fruit,
> That with exhilerating vapour bland
> About thir spirits had playd, and inmost powers
> Made err, was now exhal'd, and grosser sleep
> Bred of unkindly fumes, with conscious dreams
> Encumberd, now had left them, up they rose
> As from unrest. . . .
>
> (ix. 1046–52)

We happen to know what Milton, as theologian, believed to be the significance of the eating of the fruit. He regarded the tree of the knowledge of good and evil as merely 'a pledge, as it were, and memorial of obedience'. The tasting of its fruit was an act that included all sins: 'it comprehended at once distrust in the divine veracity, and a proportionate credulity in the assurances of Satan; unbelief, ingratitude; disobedience; gluttony; in the man excessive uxoriousness, in the woman a want of proper regard for her husband, in both an insensibility to the welfare of their offspring, and offspring the whole human race; parricide, theft, invasion of the rights of others, sacrilege, deceit, presumption in aspiring to divine attributes, fraud in the means employed to attain the object, pride, and arrogance' (*De Doctrina Christiana* I. xi, Sumner's translation). But none of this stemmed from the intoxicating power of the fruit; God was testing fidelity by forbidding 'an act of its own nature indifferent'. In other words Milton the poet establishes the theme of perturbation as a structural element in the poem, using it as an index of fallen nature, of the disaster brought upon Joy by Woe, by means which must have earned the disapproval of Milton the theologian, namely the attribution of intoxicating powers to the forbidden fruit. Joy and Woe in the poem take precedence over theological niceties; Milton's theology is in the *De Doctrina,* not in *Paradise Lost.*

Adam Unparadised

Joy and Woe, the shadow of one over the other, the passage from one to the other, are the basic topic of the poem. We turn now to Adam unparadised, to Joy permanently overshadowed by Woe, light by dark, nature by chaos, love by lust, fecundity by sterility. Death casts these shadows. It is not difficult to understand why a very intelligent Italian, reading *Paradise Lost* for the first time, should have complained to me that he had been curiously misled about its subject; for, he said, 'it is a poem about Death'.

For who would lose
Though full of pain, this intellectual being?
(ii. 146–7)

Belial asks the question, as Claudio had done; it is a human reaction, and most of the time we do not relish the thought of being without 'sense and motion' (ii. 151); nor can we help it if this is to be called 'ignoble' (ii. 227). In the same book, Milton gives Death allegorical substance, if 'substance might be calld that shaddow seemd' (669); for it is all darkness and shapelessness, a 'Fantasm' (743), all lust and anger, its very name hideous (788).

The only thing it resembles is Chaos, fully described in the same book; and it stands in relation to the order and delight of the human body as Chaos stands to Nature. So, when Satan moved out of Chaos into Nature, he not only 'into Nature brought / Miserie' (vi. 267), but into Life brought Death, and into Light (which is always associated with order and organic growth) darkness. At the end of Book ii he at last, 'in a cursed hour' (1055), approaches the pendant world, having moved towards it from Hell through Chaos; and the whole movement of what might be called the *sensuous* logic of the poem so far—the fall into darkness and disorder, the return to light and order—is triumphantly halted at the great invocation to Light which opens Book iii. But the return is of course made with destructive intent. We see the happiness of a man acquainted with the notion of Death but having no real knowledge of it—'So neer grows Death to Life, what e're Death is, / Som dreadful thing no doubt' (iv. 425–6); and then, after the long interruption of Books v–viii, which represent the everything which stretched between life and death, we witness the crucial act from which the real knowledge of Death will spring, when Eve took the fruit, 'and knew not eating Death' (ix. 792). The syntax, once again, is Greek; but we fill it with our different and complementary English senses: 'she knew not that she was eating death'; 'she knew not Death even as she ate it'; 'although she was so bold as to eat Death for the sake of knowledge, she still did not know—indeed she did not even know what she had known before, namely that this was a sin'. Above all she *eats* Death, makes it a part of her formerly incorruptible body, and so explains the human sense of the possibility of incorruption, so tragically belied by fact. The function of Death in the poem is simple enough; it is 'to destroy, or unimmortal make / All kinds' (x. 611–2). There is, of course, the theological explanation to be considered, that the success of Death in this attempt is permissive; but in terms of the poem this is really no more than a piece of dogmatic cheering-up, and Milton, as usual, allows God himself to do the explaining (x. 616 ff.). From the human point of view, the intimation of unimmortality takes priority over the intellectual comfort of God's own theodicy, simply because a man can feel, and can feel the possibility of immortality blighted.

Milton saw the chance, in Book ix, of presenting very concretely the impact of Death on Life; and it would be hard to think of a fiction more completely achieved. The moment is of Eve's return to Adam, enormously ignorant and foolishly cunning, 'with Countnance blithe. . . . But in her Cheek distemper flushing glowd' (ix. 886–7). This flush is a token of unimmortality; and then, since 'all kinds' are to be affected, the roses fade and droop in Adam's welcoming garland. He sees that Eve is lost, 'Defac't, deflowrd, and now to Death devote' (901). He retreats into Eve's self-deception; but all is lost.

The emphasis here is on *all*; from the moment of eating the fruit to that of the descent of 'prevenient grace' (end of Book x and beginning of xi) Adam and Eve have lost everything, and are, without mitigation, to death devote. If one bears this steadily in mind the tenth book is a lot easier to understand; it seems often to be misread. Adam, 'in a troubl'd Sea of passion tost' (718) cries out 'O miserable of happie!' (720) and laments the end of the 'new glorious World' (721). He feels particularly the corruption of love:

> O voice once heard
> Delightfully, *Encrease and multiply*,
> Now death to hear!
>
> (729–31)

and sums up in a couplet using the familiar pseudo-rhyme: 'O fleeting joyes / Of Paradise, deare bought with lasting woes!' (741–2). He has knowledge of the contrast between then and now, but of nothing else. Deprived of Original Justice, he is now merely natural; hence the importance of remembering that he is here simply a human being in a situation that is also simple, and capable of being felt naturally, upon our pulses. Deprived as he is, Adam finds life 'inexplicable' (754); knowing nothing of the great official plan by which good will come of all this, his speculations are by the mere light of nature. Rajan made something of this in his explanation of how Milton got his heterodox theology into the poem—mortalism, for example, is not very tendentious if proffered as the opinion of a totally corrupt man.[1] But, much more important, Adam is here for the first time true kindred to the reader. The primary appeal of poetry is to the natural man; that is why it is called simple, sensuous and passionate. When Eve

[1] B. Rajan, *Paradise Lost and the Seventeenth Century Reader* (1947), Cap ii.

proposes that they should practise a difficult abstinence in order not to produce more candidates for unimmortality, or Adam considers suicide (x. 966 ff.) we should be less conscious of their errors than of their typicality. Whatever the mind may make of it, the sensitive body continues to feel the threat of unimmortality as an outrage:

> Why is life giv'n
> To be thus wrested from us? rather why
> Obtruded on us thus? who, if we knew
> What we receive, would either not accept
> Life offerd, or soon beg to lay it down,
> Glad to be so dismisst in peace.
>
> (xi. 502–7)

Michael's treatment of the same topic that the Duke inflicts upon Claudio in *Measure for Measure* can only strengthen such sentiments:

> thou must outlive
> Thy youth, thy strength, thy beauty, which will change
> To witherd weak and gray; thy Senses then
> Obtuse, all taste of pleasure must forgo,
> To what thou hast, and for the Air of youth
> Hopeful and cheerful, in thy blood will reign
> A melancholly damp of cold and dry
> To weigh thy spirits down, and last consume
> The Baum of Life.
>
> (xi. 538–46)

Whatever the consolation offered by Death—no one would wish to 'eternize' a life so subject to distempers of every kind—it is not pretended that this makes up for the loss of the 'two fair gifts . . . Happiness / And Immortalitie' (xi. 56–8). Most criticism of the verse of Book x and xi amounts to a complaint that it is lacking in sensuousness; but this is founded on a misunderstanding of the poem. *Paradise Lost* must be seen as a whole; and whoever tries to do this will see the propriety of this change of tone, this diminution of *sense* in the texture of the verse.

A striking example of this propriety is the second of the formal salutations to Eve, Adam's in xi. 158 ff., which I have already discussed in connection with v. 385 ff. (see p. 90 above). Here Adam sees that Eve is responsible not only for death but for the victory over it; as she herself says, 'I who first brought Death on all, am grac't / The source of life' (xi. 168–9). This paradox, considered as part of the whole complex in which Milton places it, seems to me much more central to the mood of the poem than the famous *felix culpa*, because it is rooted in nature, and related to our habit of rejoicing that life continues, in spite of death, from generation to generation. Yet Adam is still under the shadow of death, and his restatement of the theme Venus-Eve-Mary is very properly deprived of the sensuous context provided for Raphael's salutation; and since the second passage cannot but recall the first, we may be sure that this effect was intended.

There, is indeed, another passage which strongly supports this view of the centrality of the paradox of Eve as destroyer and giver of life, and it has the same muted quality, casts the same shadow over the power and delight of love. This is the curious vision of the union between the sons of Seth and the daughters of Cain (xi. 556–636). The Scriptural warrant for this passage is extremely slight, though there were precedents for Milton's version. Adam rejoices to see these godly men united in love with fair women:

> Such happy interview and fair event
> Of love and youth not lost, Songs, Garlands, Flowrs
> And charming Symphonies attachd the heart
> Of *Adam*, soon enclin'd to admit delight,
> The bent of Nature. . . .
>
> (593–7)

And he thanks the angel, remarking that 'Here Nature seems fulfilld in all her ends' (602). He is at once coldly corrected; these women, against the evidence of Adam's own senses, are 'empty of all good' (616), and nothing but ill comes from the 'Sons of God' (622) yielding up all their virtue to them. Milton remembered how much of Pandora there was in Eve. From women Adam is taught to expect woe; but, more important, this change in the divine arrangements means that the evidence of the senses, the testimony of pleasure, is no longer a reliable guide:

> Judge not what is best
> By pleasure, though to Nature seeming meet . . .
> (603–4)

Paradise Lost is a poem about death, and about pleasure and its impairment. It is not very surprising that generations of readers failed to see the importance to Milton's 'scheme' of Adam's exclamation upon a paradox which depends not upon the senses but upon revelation; I mean the assurance that out of all this evil good will come as testimony of a benevolent plan

> more wonderful
> Than that which by creation first brought forth
> Light out of darkness.
> (xii. 471–3)

The senses will not recognize that out of their own destruction will come forth 'Joy and eternal Bliss' (xii. 551). In that line Milton echoes the *Comus* Epilogue—Joy will come from the great wound the senses have suffered, but it is a joy measured by what we have had and lost. And the sense of loss is keener by far than the apprehension of things unseen, the remote promise of restoration. The old Eden we know, we can describe it, inlay it with a thousand known flowers and compare it with a hundred other paradises; throughout the whole history of loss and deprivation the poets have reconstructed it with love. The new one may be called 'happier farr', but poetry cannot say much more about it because the senses do not know it. The paradise of Milton's poem is the lost, the only true, paradise; we confuse ourselves, and with the same subtlety confuse the 'simple' poem, if we believe otherwise.

Shelley spoke of Milton's 'bold neglect of a direct moral purpose', and held this to be 'the most decisive proof of the supremacy of Milton's genius'. 'He mingled, as it were', Shelley added, 'the elements of human nature as colours upon a single pallet, and arranged them in the composition of his great picture according to the laws of epic truth; that is, according to the laws of that principle by which a series of actions of the external universe and of intelligent and ethical beings is calculated to excite the sympathy of succeeding generations of mankind.'[1] This passage follows upon the famous observations on Satan, and is itself succeeded by and involved with a Shelleyan attack on Christianity; and perhaps in consequence of this it has not been thought worth much attention except by those specialized opponents who contend for and against Satan in the hero-ass controversy. Theirs is an interesting quarrel, but its ground ought to be shifted; and in any case this is not the occasion to reopen it. But the remarks of Shelley I have quoted seem to me substantially true; so, rightly understood, do the much-anathematized remarks of Blake. I say 'substantially' because Milton himself would perhaps have argued that he accepted what responsibility he could for the moral effect of his poem, and that in any case he specifically desiderated a 'fit' audience, capable of making its own distinctions between moral good and evil. Yet in so far as poetry works through the pleasure it provides—a point upon which Milton and Shelley would agree—it must neglect 'a direct moral purpose'; and in so far as it deals with the passions of fallen man it has to do with Blake's hellish energies. And however much one may feel that they exaggerated the truth in applying it to Milton, one ought to be clear that Shelley and Blake were not simply proposing naughty Romantic paradoxes because they did not know enough. Indeed they show us a truth about *Paradise Lost* which later commentary, however learned, has made less and less accessible.

With these thoughts in my mind, I sometimes feel that the shift of attention necessary to make friends out of some of Milton's most potent modern enemies is in reality a very small one. However this may be, I want to end by citing Mr. Robert Graves; not because I have any hope of persuading him from his evidently and irrationally powerful distaste for Milton, but to give myself the pleasure of quoting one of his poems. It is called 'Pure Death', and in it Mr. Graves speculates on a theme that he might have found, superbly extended, in Milton's epic:

> We looked, we loved, and therewith instantly
> Death became terrible to you and me.

[1] *A Defence of Poetry,* in *Shelley's Literary and Philosophical Criticism,* ed. J. Shawcross (1909), p. 146.

By love we disenthralled our natural terror
From every comfortable philosopher
Or tall grey doctor of divinity:
Death stood at last in his true rank and order.[1]

Milton gives us this perception, but 'according to the laws of epic truth'; which is to say, he exhibits life in a great symbolic attitude.

[1] *Collected Poems* (1959), p. 71.

VII

THE BETTER FORTITUDE

W. W. Robson

PARADISE REGAINED seems not to have received much critical attention. Perhaps this is because it is the least popular of Milton's poems. Although the poet himself 'could not endure to hear *Paradise Lost* preferred to it', no one from that day to this seems to have agreed with him. It has never attracted the same sympathetic interest as *Samson Agonistes*. And even the academic authorities who thought themselves obliged to rank it above *Comus*, and even above *Lycidas*, may well have felt that they preferred those poems. *Paradise Regained*, then, is clearly not a *tempting* poem. The very terms in which it is usually praised (as by Landor or De Quincey) suggest that it has been deferred to more than genuinely admired, and more admired than enjoyed. At the same time, *Paradise Regained* has not usually been judged to be a failure. The consensus of opinion seems to be that it is a success, though a success of a limited kind. If critics are unenthusiastic, it is not as a rule because they find in the poem a discrepancy between intention and performance. It is rather that there is felt to be something unsympathetic, something even repellent, about the intention itself.

The problem with which the poem at once confronts the reader of poetry can be suggested by quoting two passages, which when taken together are fairly representative of a contrast of modes, or qualities, pervasive in the poem.

But to guide Nations in the way of truth
By saving Doctrin, and from error lead
To know, and knowing worship God aright,
Is yet more Kingly; this attracts the Soul,
Governs the inner man, the nobler part,
That other ore the body only reigns,
And oft by force, which to a generous mind
So reigning can be no sincere delight.
Besides to give a Kingdom hath been thought
Greater and nobler don, and to lay down
Far more magnanimous than to assume.
Riches are needless then, both for themselves,
And for thy reason why they should be sought,
To gain a Scepter, oftest better miss't.

(ii. 473–86)

Have we not seen, or by relation heard,
In Courts and Regal Chambers how thou lurkst,
In Wood or Grove by mossie Fountain side,
In Valley or Green Meddow, to way-lay
Som beauty rare, *Calisto, Clymene,*
Daphne, or *Semele, Antiopa,*
Or *Amymone, Syrinx,* many more
Too long, then layst thy scapes on names ador'd,
Apollo, Neptune, Jupiter, or *Pan*,
Satyr or Fawn or Silvan? But these haunts
Delight not all; among the Sons of Men
How many have with a smile made small account
Of beauty and her lures, easily scornd
All her assaults, on worthier things intent!

(ii. 182–95)

Neither of these passages will be judged to be among the best parts of *Paradise Regained.* But the second none the less is decidedly better than the first, and it is not difficult to establish the nature of its superiority. The first passage is strangely colourless and toneless. We have the sense of a mind behind it, but we have little or no sense of a voice expressing the mind. What made it poetry for the poet? Clearly the metre—the even beat of the remarkably regular verse, with that typical monosyllabic thud at the end of so many of the lines, which, without interrupting the consecutive flow of the argument, reinforces the general effect of flat un-incantatory assertion—the effect that makes it impossible to mistake the passage for even one of the more didactic parts of *Paradise Lost*. It is this metrical movement which underlines and emphasizes the order of the poet's interests here, the stress tending to fall on demonstrative distinctions ('*this* attracts the Soul . . . *That other* ore the body only reigns') and grammatical particles ('*both* for themselves, / *And* for thy reason why they should be sought'). This assertive bent, this habit of emphasis, results in a noticeable devaluing of the quality of the emotionally toned words. Consequently, although the passage is clearly the product of strong conviction, it is virtually impossible to convey this in any vocal effect. Indeed, it is best not to try, for the attempt could only draw attention to such unfortunate effects as the last line quoted, with its clutter of dentals and sibilants, suggesting a particular intensity of spat-out or hissed-out contempt.

In comparison the second passage appears tonally much more adequate. It conveys a peculiar mixture of knowing sneer and indulged aesthetic pleasure. The second line epitomizes this effect, the voice lingering a little over 'Courts and Regal Chambers' to come down with a grimly savoured dissonance on 'lurkst'. Satan is enjoying this speech: he is *with* Belial in the 'scapes' even while he is consciously dissociating himself from them; and the lift into superiority is appropriately accompanied by a lift in the verse itself, after the pause on the long sound of 'lures', to the expression of that easy scorn.

There is nothing remarkable about the writing in the second passage; by itself it would not prompt us to analysis; it is only the contrast with the first passage that brings out how well written it is. And it may be said that there is nothing remarkable either about this kind of contrast in Milton's poetry. It seems to be accepted as matter-of-course that Milton writes better poetry for 'bad' characters than for 'good'. I am always surprised at this casual assumption about so great a poet—and none of the sensible detractors of Milton denies that he is, after all, a great poet. Yet here we have a great poet writing on a theme with which he is beyond question seriously engaged, but producing work which considered by the standards of his own best writing is inert, jejune, and dull. The problem is surely a more interesting and difficult one than the common account of the matter suggests.

For it is not always true that Milton fails to make 'good' characters speak good poetry. Here are a few lines from the Lady in *Comus*:

> Yet should I try, the uncontrouled worth
> Of this pure cause would kindle my rapt spirits
> To such a flame of sacred vehemence,
> That dumb things would be mov'd to sympathize,
> And the brute Earth would lend her nerves and shake
> Till all thy magic structures rear'd so high
> Were shattered into heaps ore thy false head.
>
> (792–98)

The motive force here is obviously an impassioned moral fervour, but in contrast with the lines of Christ quoted from *Paradise Regained* the words, the phrasing, the run of the verse, all seem to 'sympathize' with it. We feel that invoked 'shaking' in the reading, and the 'structures' (finely placed word) already unsubstantial and tottering before the last line brings them down in ruins (the alliteration of 'shake' and 'shattered' contributes to this effect of a continuous process). It is true in suggestion to say that this kind of verse is more 'dramatic' than the passage from *Paradise Regained*. But this is not because the one creates the presence of a particular dramatized *person* and the other does not. Neither is dramatic in this sense, but the passage from *Comus* employs the method of poetry, in using language to carry the mind to what it says.

It may be objected that a local dryness or dullness is not an adequate ground for condemning a long poem. But the radical criticism is that this failure in the blank verse is merely the local manifestation of an essential failure of life in the poem, and that our perception of this affects our sense of the poet's whole grasp of his theme and casts doubt upon the whole form through which he has given it expression. It is important here to avoid an elementary misunderstanding. *Paradise Regained* is certainly, in a sense, 'about something'. It is an explicitly didactic work, whose burden could be paraphrased. And on the face of it the formal outline of the poem is correspondingly clear and unambiguous.

But what criticism has to deal with here is not what would be conveyed by a prose abstract of the argument, nor by a general account of the Renaissance epic tradition in which Milton was perhaps writing. The question at issue is whether the chosen form of *Paradise Regained* corresponds in any intimate way to the chosen matter. I have here to disagree with some remarks of Mr. Northrop Frye. 'Most of us,' he says, 'tend to think of a poet's real achievement as distinct from, or even contrasted with, the achievement present in what he stole, and we are thus apt to concentrate on peripheral rather than central critical facts. For instance, the central greatness of *Paradise Regained* as a poem, is not the greatness of the rhetorical decorations that Milton added to his source, but the greatness of the theme itself, which Milton *passes on* to the reader from his source.'[1] But surely the 'passing on' of 'the greatness of the theme' is a more creative process, requires a more positive contribution from the poet, than the phrase 'passing on' by itself suggests. The great subject does not in itself make a great poem; and the only way in which we can establish relevant distinctions between *Paradise Regained* and (say) Blackmore's *Creation* is by examining everything in the poem which may be said to represent the poet's own unique sense of the theme he is handling.

The manifest undertaking to which Milton committed himself is clearly foreshadowed in the prelude to Book ix of *Paradise Lost*, where the traditional subject-matter of classical epic and chivalrous romance is rejected in favour of the epic of heroic magnanimity ('the better fortitude / Of Patience and Heroic Martyrdom'.) This promise is scarcely fulfilled in *Paradise Lost* itself, and it may be conjectured that Milton's consciousness of this played a part in his decision to write the shorter epic, in which the epic 'machinery' which occupies so much of *Paradise Lost* is drastically reduced, and the formal and the actual centring of the poem on its Hero coincide. The denial of scope to the epic 'machinery' is accompanied by a denial of elaboration to the style. This new style, at its most typical, takes its colour from the character of the Hero. He is laconic and terse. Even the actual Dominical *logia* in his mouth ('Tempt not the Lord thy God . . .' etc.) partake of this Senecan terseness. Milton's Christ (if this may be said without offence) is rude—'rude' here occupying an intermediate position

[1] *Anatomy of Criticism* (1957), p. 96.

between Othello's 'Rude am I in my speech' and the modern 'brusque, ill-mannered'. He characteristically speaks 'in brief' (iv. 485, 'So talkd he, while the Son of God went on / And stayd not'.) His more extended speeches are in the 'majestic unaffected stile' (iv. 359) which Milton attributes to the Hebrew Prophets. Satan in contrast represents the polished orator. But even he at times partakes in the new plain vocabulary and 'unpoetical' manner:

> . . . harmless, if not wholsom, *as a sneeze*
> To mans less universe.
>
> (iv. 458–9)

Compare Christ's:

> . . . collecting toys
> And trifles for choice matters, *worth a spunge*.
>
> (iv. 328–9)

This is an overflow from the manner of Milton's controversial prose. Yet the plain style, with all its laconism ('He added not . . .'), can have a certain ideal dignity of its own:

> He added not; and Satan bowing low
> His gray dissimulation, disappear'd
> Into thin Air diffus'd: for now began
> Night with her sullen wing to double-shade
> The Desert, Fowls in thir clay nests were coucht;
> And now wild Beasts came forth the woods to roam.
>
> (i. 497–502)

Even after no more than forty lines of *Paradise Regained* it becomes plain that our habit of expectation, brought over from the earlier *Paradise Lost*, of a large amplitude of sonority and grandeur of *sostenuto* is not going to be gratified. The occasional expansions in the manner of *Paradise Lost* stand out sharply in contrast with the surrounding verse:

> . . . and led thir march
> From Hells deep-vaulted Den to dwell in light,

Regents and Potentates, and Kings, yea gods
Of many a pleasant Realm and Province wide.
(i. 115–18)

Expansive 'allusions' are rare, and their orotund style seems to point to their ironic use:

Such forces met not, nor so wide a camp,
When *Agrican* with all his Northern powers
Besieg'd *Albracca,* as Romances tell . . . etc.
(iii. 337–9)

But the prevailing gravity and formality of the poem's characteristic manner forbid us any sense of having passed to a 'lower' style or a less impressive subject-matter. On the contrary, Milton's way of contrasting the new poem with the old (*ille ego qui quondam*), in the first line of *Paradise Regained*, offers the promise of a *greater* sublimity: *Paradise Lost* becomes in retrospect a song about a 'happy Garden'; the poet is now to sing of deeds 'above Heroic'. Yet until Satan's first 'undisguis'd' speech to Christ, when some sort of life begins mysteriously to stir in the verse, little or nothing is done to capture the imagination. The general impression is of a pervasive dull distinction. The frequent paraphrase of the language of the New Testament has much the same effect in Milton's stately verse as in many a sermon; the suggestiveness of the original is diluted. The landscape evoked is of the vaguest: the 'pathless Desert' into which the Son of God is led has the thinness of allegory. The style is inelastic and mannered. Milton without magniloquence, we begin to feel, is hard to read. It is against this soporific background that we hear a new note, which, in D. H. Lawrence's phrase, makes us prick our innermost ear:

'Tis true, I am that Spirit unfortunate . . .
(i. 358)

But here we are brought at once to the central peculiarity of the undertaking of *Paradise Regained.*

Milton, it has often been observed, is a striking example of that type of divided poetic personality in which the *prédilection d'artiste* for certain themes is accompanied by a moral antagonism towards them. Closely allied to this is the observation that there is apt to be a cleavage between Milton's expounded doctrines and his unconscious sympathies; and this in turn prompts the judgement that Milton's imaginative creations show a consequent tendency to 'get out of hand': Satan in *Paradise Lost*, and in a different but related way God the Father, Adam at the moment of the Fall, are said to illustrate this tendency; and the criticism has been so generally made that it might be called the characteristic adverse judgement on Milton's poetry. Now whatever general validity there may be in this criticism, it is not clear that it is at all precisely applicable to *Paradise Regained*. Whether the Satan of the later poem is or is not 'the same' character as the Satan of *Paradise Lost*, no one surely would judge that here at any rate he 'gets out of hand'. On the contrary, in the presentation of Satan as in everything else in this poem, we have the impression of the poet's measured control of his artistic intention. For example, the residual pride and self-pity of Satan in the speech just quoted (i. 357–405), so finely evoked in the tone and movement of the lines, are clearly part of the intended effect. He is presenting himself, after all, as a 'sympathetic' character:

> Men generally think me much a foe
> To all mankind: why should I? they to mee
> Never did wrong or violence
>
> (i. 387–8)

It is the detection of these arts that provokes the Saviour's 'stern' reply. But what is at issue for the reader of poetry is not the ethical content of Satan's speech or of Christ's reply, but the degree of 'presence' which the poet succeeds in bestowing on both of them. And it is impossible to judge that both are equally 'present'; this is why attempts such as that of Mr. Arnold Stein[1] to interpret the whole poem as a drama must fail. At the same time, it is equally impossible to believe that Milton was unaware of the nature of the contrast between the two speeches—of the nature of the contrast between the presentations of the two disputants generally. That contrast is too systematic, too consistent, too representative in the poem to have been unintentional. In investigating it we

[1] *Heroic Knowledge* (1957).

are led to the heart of the matter, the singularity of Milton's central purpose.

The difficulties inherent in that purpose—the presentation of Christ as the hero of an epic—can hardly be exaggerated. Certainly, 'epic' in *Paradise Regained* means something very peculiar, and it is significant that there is no real classical model for the poem—whatever encouragement for his undertaking Milton may have derived from such dubious forerunners as Vida's *Christias*.[1] Nor can neo-classical accounts of the form of certain books of the Bible have given adequate precedent. It seems to me that in its formal character *Paradise Regained* is essentially *sui generis*, and that this is consonant with Milton's sense of the unique and unrepeatable character of the Hero. (It is perhaps significant too that such typical features as the epic simile, so famously exemplified in Book i of *Paradise Lost*, do not occur in *Paradise Regained* until Book iv, and none of the similes when they do occur is at all remarkable.) But the *suggestion* of the qualities of ancient poetry is with equal certainty part of Milton's intention; in order to bring out the transcendent character of Christ's heroism, it is necessary to keep before the reader persistent reminders of the traditional heroism which Christ transcends. Now in inviting this comparison between Christ and the epic heroes Milton runs at once into a formal difficulty. In the background of comparable traditional epic is the theomachy; on the human plane the hero is the representative of a god, or of the nation favoured by the god. But in Milton's poem the uniqueness of the relationship between the hero and the god forbids even the possibility of any tension between the hero's purposes and those of the god. The whole point of the story, the ethical significance of the paradigm, is the completeness of the subordination of the hero's human purpose to the divine purpose. But respect for the central tradition of Christianity—a respect which, *pace* Saurat, Milton does nothing to disturb—rules out the imaginary evocation of an even conceivable temporary contrast between the two. The result is that Milton runs the risk of presenting Christ as a demigod, one in whom the divine and the human purposes are not so much *united* as *identical*;

[1] The nearest parallel is possibly the *Oedipus at Colonus*, and Sophocles's 'gnomic' manner may well have played a part in the formation of the style in *Paradise Regained*. But the formal relationship of the two works is far from close.

thereby not only falling into theological unorthodoxy, but emptying Christ's conduct of its exemplary character of *obedience*. It is a general point to be pondered here, whether any poet who presents the Incarnation as part of his subject does not run this risk.

But in any case this formal problem is a minor difficulty in comparison with the substantive problem Milton faced in portraying the *character* of his Hero. Now here we have at once to distinguish between superficial and essential criticisms. Those who complain that Milton's Christ is not like 'the Christ of the Gospels' must make it quite clear to themselves that they are not relying on sentimental half-memories of the Parables. They must recall the mysterious and baffling figure, so starkly presented in the gospel of Mark, and never altogether absent from the pages of the other Synoptics or of John. They must recall the 'hard sayings'. They must recall the sacred character of Christ as it has come down from the New Testament and the central tradition of Christianity—a character and a tradition which (despite once popular accusations of 'Arianism' and 'Socinianism') Milton in *Paradise Regained* nowhere abjures. But once mere sentimentality is disposed of, legitimate occasions for criticism remain. Doctrinal objections, even if they were likely to worry most modern readers, do not in my opinion arise. (The view to be found in some authors that Milton is covertly substituting the Temptation in the Wilderness for the Passion as the central mystery of Christianity is directly refutable from the text, e.g. i. 155 ff. or iv. 633–5.) The real objections are on grounds of taste and feeling, not doctrine.

It is commonly said that Milton, however doctrinally orthodox he may be shown to be in his poetry, is deeply un-Christian in feeling. Nor can this objections be brushed aside as irrelevant, since part of Milton's task as a poet is to convey the feelings appropriate to what he says. And the objections to the 'feeling' in *Paradise Regained* can be localized. The Christ who speaks of the people as 'a miscellaneous rabble' (iii. 50) is not the Christ who had compassion for the multitude. It is not simply a question of Milton's presentation being at variance with that of the gospels; for in order to assimilate Christ to his idea of the Magnanimous Man, the paragon of surly virtue, the poet has invented a detailed context for Christ's remarks, and it would be possible therefore to plead some dramatic justification for the variance. But whatever these excuses, the insensitiveness of the presentation remains. It is not possible, at these points, for Milton both to benefit from legitimate preconceptions about his Hero and to exhibit his Hero as speaking in a manner which affronts them. The error of feeling is closely related to the error of taste illustrated in Christ's discussion of the Roman worthies (iii. 443 ff.) or of the Greek philosophers (iv. 291 ff.). Here again the objection is not to the historical impossibility of these remarks—even assuming their historical impossibility. We must be prepared to grant the poet his conventions: such as making Christ speak in English blank verse. But the objection here is to imaginative incongruity. And we must go further than this. Milton's presentation of Christ, as a whole, must stand convicted of either an error of feeling or an error of taste. If he imagined that the traits of his Hero are all to be found in the historical character of Christ, he was guilty of the former; if on the other hand he supposed himself to be legitimately adding traits to it, he was guilty of the latter. It may be objected that these criticisms are not strictly relevant to a literary appraisal of *Paradise Regained*, since they depend upon the accident that Milton's poem—unlike the *Iliad* or *Aeneid*—happens to draw upon a still living religion. But this, if urged as a defence of *Paradise Regained*, is a dangerous argument. For it seems clear that the success of the poem depends upon the reader's willingness to imagine himself in sympathy with certain religious and ethical doctrines. To a reader without this sympathy, or without the capacity for it, *Paradise Regained* will be indeed a frigid work. And the fair criticism of the poem here is that Milton, by his presentation of Christ, has done something to disturb that sympathy where it already exists, and to hinder its attainment where it does not.

The conclusion is inescapable: that Milton's portrayal of Christ does not succeed in uniting the sacred figure with the epic hero. And this judgement must be associated with the criticism already passed upon the desiccation and tonelessness of so much of the verse Christ is made to speak. Both strictures regard what may be called a *failure of incarnation*. The peculiarity of *Paradise Regained* among Milton's poems is that the division of the poetic personality which prompts these strictures seems to be perfectly conscious. Milton gives all the imaginative and emotional appeal—

the characteristic appeal of poetry—to the temptations: Christ rejects them as the spokesman of pure reason. But this involves Milton in an artistic contradiction. In allowing Christ to speak poetry at all, he is obliged to supply *some* tone, *some* presence, to the voice of pure reason. The result is the acerbity in Christ's speeches which strikes the ear so disagreeably. This is the failure of incarnation in its most obvious form. Christ as the silent patient figure amid the storm conjured up by Satan is impressive. Christ's stately rudeness is less so. Imaginative temptations should be met imaginatively. The quality of feeling for a lesser good must be opposed by the quality of feeling for a higher good. To try to write poetry on another supposition is to go against the grain. It is, indeed, hard to feel that an element of penitential exercise, of deliberate self-mortification, did not enter into Milton's conception of his purpose in *Paradise Regained*. When we hear of '*Sion's* songs, to all true tastes excelling', we cannot but recall that Milton's one undoubted failure as a poet is his own translation of Psalms. And the note of the famous passage on Athens (iv. 237) is unmistakable. It is the note of love; not that intimate love for a particular actual place that sounds in the great choral ode of Sophocles, but the bookish man's love, no less real and longing, for an ideal country of the mind. The reply of Christ is not even intellectually satisfying. Who can listen without irritation to the scholar-poet evolving the ingenious paradox (iv. 321–5) whereby reading is discredited? But what is really objectionable is the note of feeling. The fine-writing of the passage on Athens, and the speech of Christ which rejects it, seem both self-indulgences—indulgences of different 'selves', different habits of feeling, in the poet.

The more successful parts of *Paradise Regained* depend on a more equivocal relation between Milton the artist and Milton the moralist. As a moralist, Milton deals in simple heroic opposites: good against evil; temptation and rejection; to stand or to fall. The climax of the poem, when Christ miraculously is sustained upon the pinnacle of the Temple, epitomizes this grand simplicity:

> To whom thus *Jesus*: Also it is written,
> Tempt not the Lord thy God: he said, and stood.
> But *Satan* smitten with amazement fell.
>
> (iv. 560 ff.)

Good and evil are confronted: good stands and evil falls. Such is the bare *schema* of the poem. But who can feel that the actual Satan of the poem is 'evil'? However discredited and contemned, he is 'serviceable to Heaven's King' by Christ's own admission. He is even a Son of God; the title, as he employs it polemically, has a terrible irony; but at one moment (iii. 203 ff.) the tragedy of the rejected Son beside the 'Son beloved', allowing himself to dream of Christ's intercession with their common Father, is fully realized. This dramatizing of the figure of Satan raises the story above the level of a mere debate. Satan is made 'serviceable' to the poet: it is in Satan's language, rather than in anything Milton directly tells us about Christ, that we feel the *attractiveness* of heroic virtue. Yet Milton does not allow the dramatization of the suffering Adversary to conflict with his function as the Tempter. Rather, the personal appeal of Satan is made to reinforce the temptations.

> If I then to the worst that can be haste,
> Why move thy feet so slow to what is best . . .?
>
> (iii. 224–5)

Satan is the servant of Milton's art. That is, I think, why his 'evil' remains in the poem merely schematic, nominal. Milton required, more than most poets, a positive feeling for what he was writing about. A certain *uncritical* element in his genius is at once his strength and his weakness. It is the weakness that we chiefly see in *Paradise Regained.* Every reader notices the close relationship, amounting virtually to identification, between Milton—or one side of Milton—and his Hero. A rigid, uncompromising angularity is set up as the standard of value. Surely—apart from the error of taste involved in making Christ impersonate it—so *simpliste* a procedure is open to criticism. The Hero at the worst moments of the poem is made to sound like an irritable snob: but Milton, owing to the uncritical simplicity of the moral position he had adopted, has no means of avoiding this. It was a tactical mistake to confine courtesy to the Devil. There is a certain guilelessness here which reminds us that Milton belonged spiritually to the age of Spenser, not that to Dryden. He has no sense of the dangers inherent in so unqualified an identification between the Hero's righteousness and his own.

'Si fort qu'on soit, on peut éprouver le besoin de s'incliner devant quelqu'un ou quelque chose. S'incliner devant Dieu, c'est toujours le moins humiliant.' I wish I could feel that the Milton of *Paradise Regained* had been capable of such a reflection.

VIII

PARADISE REGAINED
A DISSENTIENT APPENDIX

F. W. Bateson

AT MR. ROBSON'S own invitation I add an 'Oxford' supplement to his acute and persuasive statement of what I take to be the contemporary 'Cambridge' position.

The essential difference between us lies perhaps in a concealed aesthetic premise. To Mr. Robson (p. 127 above) 'the method of poetry' is 'using language to carry the mind to the things it expresses'. But is it? I should have thought that was the method of prose. A poem, on the contrary, uses language to carry the mind from the *things* expressed, i.e. extra-social reality, to the *modes of their expression* (the best words in the best order). To a Cambridge critic it is a matter of little or no importance—or so it seems—whether the literary artifact is poetic or prosaic provided that the stuff and weight of human experience are somehow communicated. But to the strict Oxford sect—though Mr. Robson teaches at Oxford his Cambridge sympathies are no secret—the prose-poetry antithesis is absolute. Prose can be translated; poetry is what the poem loses in translation, what it *must* lose since the poetic modes of expression are a refined extrapolation of a particular society at a particular moment in its history.

The issue, endemic in all Milton criticism, comes to a head in *Paradise Regained,* because the non-stylistic content—here I am in complete agreement with Mr. Robson—is so perfunctory and unsympathetic. But poetically (after all *Paradise Regained* proclaims itself on the original titlepage 'A Poem. In IV *Books*') the words and the word-order exist in a dimension of their own. The theme implicit in a poem's style may even contradict the overt dramatic or narrative theme it is supposed to be expressing; the notorious case is that of Spenser, who it will be remembered was Milton's 'Original'. And there are undeniable poets like Akenside, Campbell, Swinburne and Dylan Thomas, in whom the *only* significance seems to be one of style. *Paradise Regained* is no doubt more than a virtuoso performance, but its virtuosity—in the best passages a supreme virtuosity—is the first point an Oxford critic will wish to make. For Hopkins, whose scattered comments add up to a remarkably complete and consistent interpretation of Milton, *Paradise Regained* was 'an advance' in Milton's 'art' over *Paradise Lost* (letter to R. W. Dixon, 5 Oct. 1878). And the 'art' Hopkins had in mind was not just the Counterpoint Rhythm or balance of speech rhythm and iambic pattern, but also included a mastery both of 'the sequence of phrase' and of 'the current language heightened' (letters to Dixon and Robert Bridges, 13 June 1878 and 14 Aug. 1879).

The first paragraph of Book i exemplifies the poem's typical style (my punctuation, repeated words in italics):

> I who e're while the happy Garden *sung*,
> *By one mans* dis*obedience* lost, now *sing*
> Recover'd Paradise to *all* mankind,
> *By one mans* firm *obedience*, fully tri'd
> Through *all tempt*ation, and the *Tempter* foil'd
> In *all* his wiles, defeated and repuls't,
> And Eden rais'd in the waste Wilderness.

Even a casual reader is unlikely to miss (1) the speeding up of the rhythm enforced by the absence of a genuine caesura in lines 3 and 7; (2) the counterpoise of caesuras after the first and eighth syllables respectively in lines 1 and 2; (3) the long or heavy sounds at the ends of lines 1 to 6 ('You will find that Milton pays much attention to consonant-quality or gravity of sound in his line endings,' Hopkins to Dixon, 14 Jan. 1881); (4) the consequent fading-away effect of the three short vowels in the last word of the paragraph ('Wilderness'); (5) the impression of solidification or concretion achieved by the series of verbal repetitions as well as the repetition of idea in 'happy Garden', 'Paradise' and 'Eden'; (6) the persistent alliteration and assonance (note especially the half-rhyme of 'rais'd in' and 'waste Wild . . .' in line 7). And the technical catalogue could be continued into word-lengths, degrees and varieties of connotation (especially 'happy Garden' and 'waste Wilderness'), the metaphoric ambiguity of 'rais'd' (line 7), etc. But this sort of pigeon-holing soon becomes tedious, because to be fully efficacious the various devices must all ring in the reader's head at the same time. The curious exhilaration a control over language as supreme as Milton's extorts is induced above all by the apparent *simultaneity* of the explosions at the various levels of sound and sense.

I agree the baroque magnificence of *Paradise Lost*'s first paragraph (26 lines) does make *Paradise Regained*'s 7 lines look rather drab and unenterprising. But the numerical ratio is approximately that of 12 books to 4, and it is permissible to prefer to the precarious magnificence of *P.L.*, the long paragraphs only just holding together, the more assured *P.R.*. Thus the long mythological passage in Satan's retort to Belial, which Mr. Robson quotes at the beginning of his essay seems to me a triumph of the middle or pastoral style. And the final paragraph of Book i, which Mr. Robson quotes, is supremely satisfying to me in its condensed and laconic art. Note how the sarcastic polysyllables 'dissimulation', 'disappear'd', and 'diffus'd' echo each other and also contrast with 'thin air' (with its suggestion of Prospero), and then how the bold and sophisticated 'double-shade' fades out in the Blakean

> And now wild Beasts came forth the woods to roam.

The passage spans a whole range of English poetic style from Sidney to Keats. No one would claim that there are more than 50 lines of quite this quality in the rest of *P.R.*, but their stylistic brilliance arises from—is, indeed, a function of—their context. Encouraged by the realization the reader whose principal concern is the poetry will accept as a necessary preparatory discipline, not without its own occasional rewards, the bare ascetic style in which they are framed.

IX

THE SUBLIME ART
NOTES ON MILTON AND HÖLDERLIN

Michael Hamburger

The first thing to be said is that all the rules of criticism forbid this comparison between two poets as incommensurable in kind, period, nationality and personal temper as Milton and Hölderlin, who were not even linked by an immediate influence, far less by borrowings that would provide a solid and respectable basis for the attempt. The differences between Milton and Hölderlin are blatantly obvious; their affinities are real, but so impalpable as to call for crude categories and dubious generalizations. What is still more discouraging, a full investigation of these affinities would require a great deal more learning than I possess; not only specialized knowledge of both Milton and Hölderlin scholarship, but an encyclopaedic general knowledge too forbidding to outline. If the gulf that divides the two poets can be bridged at all, however flimsily, these notes may provoke others to apply the necessary equipment. Meanwhile it may prove of some value merely to survey and measure the gulf; to establish the extent and nature of the differences without losing sight of the affinities.

*   *   *   *   *

A start was made by Dr. L. S. Salzberger in her monograph on Hölderlin[1] in which she traced the 'typical Renaissance view

[1] L. S. Salzberger: *Holderlin* (1952), pp. 8–12.

of the *poeta theologus* or *sacer vates*', and concluded: 'Hölderlin was himself one of the poets who embodied the Renaissance ideal. His spiritual forbears were Vida, Tasso, Ronsard and Sidney, as well as Milton and Klopstock. All these poets belong to the period which began with the Renaissance and ended some time after the French Revolution'. Hölderlin owed his participation in the Renaissance tradition to the German writers who influenced him in his youth, especially Klopstock and Herder, but also to his education at Denkendorf, Maulbronn and Tübingen, with their emphasis on the harmonious blending of theological and classical studies. As Dr. Salzberger mentions, the inner gate of the Protestant Seminary at Tübingen bore the inscription *Aedes Deo et Musica Sacrae*. So much for spiritual genealogy. To enter into the peculiarities of Swabian theology, or Hölderlin's possible debt to the millenarian and mystical doctrines of Bengel or Oetinger would be to plunge into the gulf with little hope of ever emerging; but even here certain interesting genealogical convergences and divergences with Milton might well be revealed. Essentially, the Swabian tradition insists that the glory of God is manifested in nature.[1]

If Hölderlin had been born some twenty years earlier than he was, Milton would almost certainly have been one of his masters. Kant's admiration for Milton is well known; even Goethe, born twenty-five years after Kant and twenty-one years before Hölderlin, had read Milton by the time he was seventeen, in 1766. The first three books of *Paradise Lost* had been translated into German as early as 1678; the Latin translation by Hog followed in 1690. But it was in the half-century between 1720 and 1770, the year of Hölderlin's birth, that Milton's example was of crucial importance to Germany. The advocacy of French classicism as the chief exemplar for German writers was effectively opposed from three directions; that of classical antiquity, that of bardic or folk poetry and that of modern English literature. To Gottsched's emphasis on discursive logic, correct usage and pedantic good sense, the

[1] Hölderlin's debt to the Swabian theologians has been investigated by Herbert Wocke: *Hölderlins Christliches Erbe* (1949). Robert Minder has written a brilliant summary of a tradition which he traces not only to Hölderlin, but to Hegel and Karl Marx. See his '"*Herlichkeit*" *chez Hegel ou Le Monde des Pères Souabes*', Etudes Germaniques, July–December 1951, pp. 225–90.

two Swiss critics Bodmer and Breitinger opposed the view that 'a well-cultivated imagination distinguishes the good poet from the vulgar versifier because it is the rich, modulating poetry, which derives its life and character from the imagination alone, that chiefly distinguishes poetry from prose'. This 'rich modulating poetry' was none other than Milton's. From 1724 to 1754 Bodmer worked at three consecutive translations of *Paradise Lost*, all of them in prose but designed to approximate more and more closely to Milton's poetry. In 1741 Bodmer published a defence of Milton, *On the Marvellous in Poetry*, closely related to Breitinger's earlier treatise on the peculiar logic of poetry, which proceeds by 'images of sensible objects'.

Bodmer and Breitinger liberated German poetry much as Lessing liberated German drama; and Milton was their battle-cry, as Shakespeare and the Greek dramatists were Lessing's. Bodmer's translation of *Paradise Lost* inspired Klopstock with the ambition to write his *Messias*. 'To judge by this fragment, Milton's spirit rests upon the poet', was Bodmer's comment on the early prose version of the first three cantos, which Klopstock submitted to him. Bodmer's enthusiasm was such that he invited Klopstock to be his guest in Switzerland. Because of the wide acceptance of Bodmer's and Klopstock's own belief that he had done for Germany what Milton had done for England, it was Klopstock's, not Milton's, epic that Hölderlin read and imitated in his formative years, in the seventeen-eighties. One other translation of *Paradise Lost* had appeared in 1760; but this German rendering by Zachariä in the modified classical hexameters which Klopstock chose for the final version of his *Messias*, was the last to appear before Milton's replacement by Klopstock in Germany.[1] The complete *Messias* was published in 1773. Milton continued to be read by Germans of the older generation, or by those with a special interest in English literature, but his general influence rapidly declined.

It will be impossible here to trace the development that divides Klopstock from Milton; the reduction of cosmology to inwardness, the substitution of enthusiasm for Milton's vast range of

[1] A few allusions in Hölderlin's early poems suggest that he may have read, or at least glanced at, Zachariä's translation, as Professor Paul Böckmann has pointed out to me; but no evidence for this assumption has yet been published.

learned allusion, scientific as well as theological and mythological. Once again it is convenient to take refuge in 'the Renaissance ideal'. From his adolescence onwards, Hölderlin aimed at a synthesis characteristic of this ideal. At Tübingen he wrote an essay on the parallels between the Proverbs of Solomon and Hesiod's *Works and Days*. Milton's account of his aspirations in the Preface to Book II of *The Reason of Church Government* applies almost equally to Hölderlin's: 'That what the greatest, choicest wits of Athens, Rome, or modern Italy, and those Hebrews of old did for their country, I, in my proportion, with this over and above, of being a Christian, might do for mine'. So does his comparison of himself in the same Preface with Jeremiah and Tiresias; but the closest analogy of all occurs in the following passage: 'The Scripture also affords us a divine pastoral drama in the Song of Solomon, consisting of two persons, and a double chorus, as Origen rightly judges. And the Apocalypse of St. John is the majestic image of a high and stately tragedy, shutting up and intermingling her solemn scenes and acts with a sevenfold chorus of hallelujahs and harping symphonies . . . Or if occasion shall lead, to imitate those magnific odes and hymns, wherein Pindarus and Callimachus are in most things most worthy . . .' The Apocalypse and Pindar's odes are the very two works which Hölderlin emulated in his prophetic 'hymns'.

Because of his syncretism, it could be said of Hölderlin, as of Milton, that 'he had his thoughts constantly fixed on the contemplation of Hebrew theocracy, and of a perfect commonwealth', though it was the theocracy of an idealized Greece that Hölderlin much more frequently invoked; and, as Hazlitt also observed of Milton, that 'his religious zeal infused its character into his imagination, so that he devotes himself with the same sense of duty to the cultivation of his genius, as he did to the exercise of virtue, or the good of his country'. To these attributes of the *sacer vates* we can add the religious radicalism that prevented both men from making a profession of their vocation, though both were intended for the Church; both were mainly deterred by 'a conscience that would retch', though their more specific reasons for preferring 'a blameless silence' were far from identical. Milton at one time chose to be 'degraded to a schoolmaster', as Johnson put it; and for the greater part of his active life Hölderlin was reduced to the drudgery and servitude of a private tutor, although, at least in youth, he also shared Milton's political radicalism.

The *sacer vates*, as such, is intransigent and incorruptible. If he tends towards one sin or excess, that sin or excess is pride, a pride as far removed from mere social or moral convention as his egregious ambition. Milton and Hölderlin are personally incommensurable because Hölderlin's vocational pride conflicted with the humility and tenderness of his nature. Indeed, his late poetry is pervaded by the anguish that sprang from the recognition of this pride as the sin of *hubris*. Because Milton does not appear to have suffered any such conflict or recognition, he remains personally aloof from us moderns, if not personally loathsome, monstrous, 'inhuman'—and this despite the egotism on which Coleridge remarked, adding that 'the egotism of such a man is a revelation of the spirit'. We can understand Hölderlin's strength and forgive his pride because he was aware of his weakness, and this awareness entered into his work. I shall have more to say of this difference, which is not one of personality alone.

Hölderlin's brief poetic career was a perpetual crisis, a perpetual revision of the premisses and functions of the *sacer vates*. For that reason, his work cannot be classified as a whole. He began by being 'not a picturesque, but a musical poet', as Coleridge said of Milton, with the musical poet's leaning towards generality and abstraction. The distinction of course is one of degree rather than of kind; one doubts whether it would have occurred to any reader of Milton who was not familiar with Shakespeare. Hazlitt denied its relevance to Milton, but Mr. Eliot's essays took it up again with a vengeance. Within a few years Hölderlin's poetry underwent a complete transformation; the visual sense became increasingly important to him; and, with it, the particular image.[1] From being at least as abstract a poet as his immediate exemplars, Klopstock and Schiller, Hölderlin became one of the most concrete and sensuous by the time of his mental breakdown and the pure imagism of *Hälfte des Lebens*. To understand this development it would be necessary to refer once more to the mystical realism of the Swabian theological tradition. Whatever its causes, it is this development, as well as the difference

[1] The various drafts of his ode *Des Morgens* (1799) show how 'the leaves of the trees' becomes 'the poplar bends', then 'the birch-tree bends', finally 'the beech-tree bends'.

in kind between *Paradise Lost* and Hölderlin's predominantly lyrical and choric poetry, that makes it impossible to compare the two poets' work as a whole. Only Milton's *Samson* and Hölderlin's *Empedocles* are sufficiently close to each other in kind to permit a valid comparison; and one would expect even this comparison to illumine little more than the vicissitudes and decline of the *sacer vates* in 'an age of dearth'.[1]

* * * * *

A few preliminary observations must be made. In his recent history of Hölderlin criticism,[2] Professor Alessandro Pellegrini summed up the crucial difference between Hölderlin and his predecessors—Milton, Dante, Sophocles and Pindar are those whom he mentions—by observing that 'Hölderlin's world was one in which he alone believed'. Whereas for Milton 'poetic vision was a symbol of theological reality and the testimony of a communal faith, of an "Ecclesia" and the spiritual unity of a people', Hölderlin 'spoke to a chorus that could not respond to him, because it did not exist'. There is a good deal of truth in this historical view; but I sometimes suspect that we exaggerate the isolation of poets close to us in time, and invent a mythical state of community for poets more remote. It has always been in the nature of a prophet to be without honour not only in his own country, but in his own time. Milton's personal, and even literary, isolation in his later years was hardly less extreme than Hölderlin's before his madness; and his 'Ecclesia', like Hölderlin's, was largely invisible. Neither Milton nor Hölderlin could become wholly identified with any political or sectarian cause; and for much the same reasons.

Without going as far as Denis Saurat, who speaks of Milton's pantheistic ideas[3] and discovers a host of heterodox beliefs that were certainly Hölderlin's, if they were not Milton's, one cannot help being struck by certain basic assumptions common to the two poets. One of these can be summed up by Saurat's statement about Milton that 'the early days before the Fall will become for him the

[1] Hölderlin: *Brod und Wein,* VII '. . . wozu Dichter in dürftiger Zeit?'

[2] Alessandro Pellegrini: *Hölderlin–Storia della Critica* (1956), pp. 414–15.

[3] Denis Saurat: *Milton–Man and Thinker* (1944), pp. 13–14, and *passim.*

normal state of a man'.[1] This is the 'concord and law of nature' of *Paradise Lost* (Book xii, 29), the peace whose loss Hölderlin laments in his ode *Der Frieden*, ending with the prayer:

Komm du nun, du der heiligen Musen all,
Und der Gestirne Liebling, verjüngender
Ersehnter Friede, komm' und gieb ein
Bleiben im Leben, ein Herz uns wieder.

Now come, belovèd of all the Muses and
The circling constellations, O long desired
Rejuvenator, Peace, and give us
Back a firm foothold in life, a centre.

It is true that Milton's Michael says a little later in the same speech:

Tyrannie must be,
Though to the Tyrant thereby no excuse—
(xii. 95–6)

a realization of the necessity of evil that also runs through Hölderlin's later poems; but it remains equally true that the *sacer vates* can approve nothing but perfection. 'Milton,' Saurat also comments,[2] 'will think that the best government is that which governs least'; and, after his disillusionment with the revolutionary cause, in a letter of 1801, Hölderlin wrote: 'In the end it is still true, that the less men discover and know about the State, whatever its form, the freer they are.'

In his early *Tractate of Education* Milton professed that 'the end of learning is to repair the ruin of our first parents . . .' To Hölderlin, writing after Rousseau and Herder, the problem presented itself not in terms of sin and redemption, but of nature and art—art in its wider Renaissance sense which embraced all that we now call culture and civilization; granted his greater emphasis on this antinomy, which worried Goethe and Schiller also, his aspirations were akin to Milton's. 'There are two ideals

[1] *Ibid.*, p. 56. But the statement is a half-truth at the most. Surely the turning-point of *Paradise Lost,* on the human level at least, is Adam's change of heart in Book X, when he ceases to blame Eve and accepts the consequences of the Fall.

[2] *Op. cit.*, p. 53.

of our existence,' Hölderlin wrote in 1794, 'a state of extreme ingenuousness, in which our needs themselves are in concord, both with our abilities and with everything related to us, solely through the organization of nature, without our interference; and a state of extreme culture, where the same would take place with infinitely multiplied, varied and intensified needs and abilities, through the organization which we are able to give to ourselves'.[1]

Like Hölderlin, though not as constantly or emphatically, Milton vindicated the 'faultless proprieties of nature', 'the faultless innocence of nature'; and the most 'artificial' of English poets wrote in *The Apology for Smectymnuus*: 'For doubtless that according to art is most eloquent, which turns and approaches nearest to nature from whence it came; and they express nature best, who in themselves least wander from her safe leading, which may be called regenerate reason.' To Hölderlin art was 'the bloom and perfection of nature'.[2] In his short preface to the hymn *Friedensfeier* he apologized as follows for the unconventional and difficult manner of his late poems: 'On a fine day almost every mode of song makes itself heard; and nature, whence it originates, also receives it again.'

These affinities must be noted, though they are tenuous without an account of the theological and philosophical premisses that divide the two poets, but especially the polytheism and pantheism of Hölderlin's earlier work. One must distinguish between a purely artistic insight in Milton, related to his famous (and usually misquoted) dictum that poetry is 'more simple, sensuous and passionate 'than rhetoric, and Hölderlin's fervent faith in the regenerative power of nature. Here Milton is 'naïve' and Hölderlin 'sentimental', according to Schiller's distinction. The modern feeling for nature, Schiller pointed out, 'is not that which the ancients had; rather it is similar to that which we have for the ancients'. It is only when Paradise is lost that Adam invokes its scenery in the pathetic mode of Hölderlin's odes and elegies:

> O Woods, O Fountains, Hillocks, Dales and Bowrs,
> With other echo late I taught your Shades
> To answer, and resound farr other Song.
>
> (x. 860–2)

[1] Hölderlin: Preface to the *Hyperion* fragment of 1794.

[2] Hölderlin: *Grund zum Empedokles*.

The same is true of the great pantheistic climax of Hölderlin's novel, *Hyperion*, with its resolution of every conflict and division in the One and All of nature: 'Men drop from you like rotten fruit, oh, let them perish, and to your root they shall return, and I, O Tree of Life, let me grow verdant again with you and waft around your crests with all your burgeoning twigs! Peaceful and closely akin, for all of us grew up out of the golden seed-grain.' It is not till the loss of Eden that Adam and Eve will be consoled by the thought of their unity with the maternal substance, which in Hölderlin is not separated from the male principle, 'spirit', 'ether' and 'light', and Milton's Michael does not take the sting out of death when he touches on this corporeal return, because it is far from being spiritual redemption:

> So mayst thou live, till like ripe Fruit thou drop
> Into thy Mothers lap, or be with ease
> Gatherd, not harshly pluckt, for death mature . . .
>
> (x. 535–7)

Saurat writes of Milton that 'for him the body and soul came to be one';[1] but even Hölderlin found it increasingly difficult to maintain this premiss, crucial though it is to his earlier work.

Nor is there any real and immediate connection between the doctrine of 'retraction' which Saurat (incorrectly, some say) attributes to Milton, and Hölderlin's belief in the alternation of 'day' and 'night', divine revelation and divine absence. The dazzling brightness which in Milton is the timeless quality of both the Father and the Son, even when their full blaze is diffused through a cloud (*P.L.* iii. 372–89), is subject to a cyclic process in Hölderlin, depending on the capacity of mortals to endure the light of revelation. The only possible parallel occurs in Book xii, when Michael forecasts an era of utter retraction:

> Thus will the latter, as the former World,
> Still tend from bad to worse, till God at last
> Wearied with thir iniquities, withdraw
> His presence from among them, and avert
> His holy Eyes;
>
> (105–9)

[1] *Op. cit.*, p. 49.

But this era is not the one to which Hölderlin alludes in his elegy *Brod und Wein,* viii, when 'the Father averted His face from mankind, and all over the earth sorrowing, rightly, began'. Hölderlin means the era between the decline of Hellas and the birth of Christ; and he sees his own age as a similar era of darkness that will end only with the joint epiphany of Christ and the ancient gods. Before his late hymns, Hölderlin's cosmological vision recalls the pre-Socratic philosophers, and particularly Empedocles, because it derives from the cycles of nature, not from history in the Christian sense. The precise relation between Christ and the gods of Greece will be the subject of his later prophetic hymns; and it is only gradually that Christ becomes more than the 'genius' of *Brod und Wein*, more than one of many mediators—including the demi-gods, prophets and poets of antiquity—between mortals and 'the God of gods', the supreme and timeless deity.

Even Hölderlin's chiliasm rests on a tradition, though a tradition more esoteric than that on which Milton mainly drew. Neither, intrinsically, was a popular poet. If *Paradise Lost* found its way into thousands of English nonconformist homes, Hölderlin's poems, by a rather different posthumous development, found their way into the packs of thousands of German soldiers in the Second World War. A special 'field selection' was issued for this purpose in 1943, the centenary year of Hölderlin's death. But what an irony! It is as though British soldiers had been provided with copies of Milton's *Areopagitica* so that they could read: 'What does He do then but reveal Himself to His servants, and as His manner is, first to His Englishmen?' Milton's messianic patriotism is related to that which inspired a number of Hölderlin's late hymns dedicated to Swabia, the Rhine and Germany respectively. These three prophetic hymns were duly included in the 'field selection'. But what were Hitler's soldiers to make of the conclusion of *Germania*?

> . . . Germania, wo du Priesterin bist
> Und wehrlos Rat giebst rings
> Den Königen und den Völkern.

> . . . Germania, where you are priestess
> And weaponless proffer advice
> To the kings and the peoples around you.

In view of such historical realities, it is not the isolation of the modern *sacer vates*, but his fame, that seems anomalous. If we add that Hölderlin had to contend with the secular philosophy of his time, the subjective, if not solipsistic idealism of Kant's successors, we can appreciate the difference between the dilemmas of Milton's Samson and Hölderlin's Empedocles. It is a triple estrangement, from the gods, from society and from himself, that defeats the protagonist of Hölderlin's unfinished tragedy.

* * * * *

The two works are commensurable only because both derive from what Milton called 'Attic tragedies of stateliest and most regal argument'. Hölderlin, it is true, was less concerned with stateliness, the classical decorum which had been replaced in his time and country by the starkness of unadorned emotion; he anticipated Nietzsche in recognizing the 'dionysian' character of the ancient Greeks, in seeing them dialectically as acquiring 'Junonian sobriety' just because, innately, they inclined to 'holy drunkenness' or 'holy pathos'. The modern 'occidental' poet, who is colder and more sober by nature, must reverse this dialectic process. What is tragic in modern times is 'that we leave the realm of the living quite calmly, packed into a container, not that devoured by flames we atone for the flame which we could not master'.[1] In his later commentary on his translation of *Oedipus Rex*, published in 1804, Hölderlin gave the following definition of ancient tragedy: 'The representation of the tragic is mainly based on this: that what is monstrous and terrible in the coupling of god and man, so that they are one at the moment of wrath, should be made intelligible by showing how this fusion into one is purged by their total separation.' Both Milton and Hölderlin rendered much of the outer form and structure of Greek tragedy; but Milton, who in any case modelled himself on Euripides, not on Sophocles, appears to have emulated its gravity and morality rather than the mystery of which Hölderlin wrote. Yet Goethe said to Eckermann that *Samson Agonistes* is 'closer to the spirit of the ancients than any other play by any modern poet whatever' (Jan. 31, 1830).

Goethe also mentioned that 'Milton's own blindness proved a great advantage to him in rendering Samson's condition with such verisimilitude'. In fact it is the rare degree to which both Milton's

[1] Hölderlin: *Letter to Böhlendorf*, December 1801.

Samson and Hölderlin's Empedocles are identified with their authors, so that these works can be interpreted either as tragedies or as elaborate *personae*, that casts so much light on my present theme. Like Coleridge, both Goethe and Schiller were also acutely aware of Milton's personality in *Paradise Lost*. Just as Coleridge stressed the subjectivity of *Paradise Lost*, remarking that 'in all modern poetry in Christendom there is an under-consciousness of a sinful nature, a fleeting away of external things, the mind or subject greater than the object, the reflective character predominant', Schiller wrote to Goethe: 'In this poem too, as with all modern works of art, it is really the individual manifested in it that arouses our interest. The topic is abominable, outwardly plausible, but inwardly worm-eaten and hollow . . . But certainly it is an interesting man who speaks . . . Indeed, the strange, unique case that, as a revolutionary come to grief, he (Milton) is better able to assume the rôle of the devil than that of the angel, has a great influence upon the characterization and structure of the poem, as the circumstance of the author's blindness has upon its tone and colouring'.[1] But Milton criticism in the late eighteenth and nineteenth centuries shows how each writer projects his own subjectivity, and his own beliefs, on to Milton's poem; with *Samson* we are on slightly firmer ground.

The very choice of their respective heroes reveals the gulf between Milton and Hölderlin. We know what Milton thought of Hölderlin's hero, because he placed him in the Paradise of Fools:

> . . . he who to be deemd
> A God, leap'd fondly into *Aetna* flames
> *Empedocles* . . .

in the company of

> Embryoes and Idiots, Eremits and Friers
> White, Black and Grey, with all thir trumperie.
> (*P.L.* iii. 469–75)

Doubtless Milton would have thought as little of Hölderlin's Empedocles, with his modern sensibility and tenderness added

[1] Schiller to Goethe, July 31st, 1799; he goes on to criticize Milton's preoccupation with free will. Goethe's reply of August 3rd is also critical of the poem, on different grounds, and also concludes that Milton remains 'an excellent, and in every way an interesting man'.

to pagan heresies, as he did of the historical. Hölderlin, on the other, might have thought Milton's hero just a little bit smug, a little bit priggish even, and more than a little barbaric. The short chorus in praise of Samson's temperance (541–46) would have struck him as wholly contrary to the spirit of Greek tragedy, if not as ludicrous as Milton thought Empedocles; and he would scarcely have sympathized with the manner in which Samson justifies 'the ways of God to men', not only because here 'the moment of wrath' is also the moment of indiscriminate slaughter —and Hölderlin's sensibility was Christian, even when his beliefs were not—but because it might have seemed to him that Samson's *hubris* is not sufficiently purged by 'total separation' from his God. Samson's outward pride remains unbroken, as the scene with Dalila shows; and so does his immense egotism, the 'alcohol of egotism' which Coleridge discovered in Milton's Satan and 'all the mighty hunters of mankind from Nimrod to Napoleon', these 'great men as they are called'. But Hölderlin would have been less interested in these relatively superficial aspects than in Milton's treatment of the tragic crux; and this he would undoubtedly have approved and admired.

Milton's Samson and Hölderlin's Empedocles have this in common, that—like the *sacer vates* himself—they are the elect of God, called and chosen for a unique mission. In the pantheistic terms that were Hölderlin's at the time, this means not so much an identification with the will of God, as the 'awareness of being at one with all that lives', the 'intellectual point of view' of which a tragic poem is the 'metaphor'.[1] Samson's physical prowess has its counterpart in Empedocles' political power and influence over the people of Agrigentum, though this power is far less important to him than its source, the divine favours bestowed on him. What the Philistines are to Samson, the rulers of his own State are to Empedocles, though this external opposition, too, ceases to be of great account in the late version, since Empedocles has condemned himself even more rigorously than his enemies condemn him. In Hölderlin's original plan for the tragedy, drafted in 1797, there is no mention of Empedocles' guilt at all, only of his 'hatred for culture'—culture as opposed to nature—his 'contempt for any very definite occupation' and for 'any interest directed towards

[1] Hölderlin: *Über den Unterschied zwischen lyrischer, epischer und und tragischer Dichtung*. Works (Zinkernagel), ii, 368–76.

diverse ends', rather than 'the great harmony with all that lives'. Pride is implied, but not censured. According to this early plan, Empedocles was also to be provoked by the sarcasms of his wife into leaving Agrigentum and seeking solitude near Etna—a detail of the plot that would have appealed to Milton, but was never carried out by Hölderlin. The earliest fragment of the play stresses the conflict between Empedocles and the representatives of the religious and political *status quo*. The citizens of Agrigentum even offer to make Empedocles their king, but with the noble scorn of the *sacer vates* for anything less than Heaven on earth, the divine republic, he declines the honour. 'The time of kings is past,' he says, and tells them to be ashamed of themselves for wanting a king.

But in 1799 Hölderlin attempted a second version of *The Death of Empedocles*; though very much more fragmentary than the first, this conforms to his deeper insights into the nature of tragedy. The last of the three fragments, *Empedocles on Etna*, is a magnificent poem, but hardly a dramatic one; written in 1800, it belongs to Hölderlin's prophetic phase and has an impersonal grandeur which transcends tragedy. Empedocles, in fact, has become a seer as far above political conflict as above personal guilt. It is the second fragment, therefore, which concerns me here.

Unlike the earlier plan and the first version, the second opens with the hero's 'separation', like Milton's tragedy, though Empedocles' external downfall has not yet been brought about by Hermocrates, the priest, and Mecades, the archon, who plot it in the first scene. In this way Hölderlin at once establishes a tragic irony not unlike that in *Samson*, for Empedocles is beyond them, as Samson is beyond Dalila, Harapha and even Manoah—only more so. Samson has his chorus instead to give him moral solace and support. A chorus of Agrigentines was part of Hölderlin's scheme, but it is significant that he failed to make use of it in any of the fragments. In the first version of *The Death of Empedocles* the function of the chorus has to be taken over by the archon's daughter, Panthea, who comments chorus-like on Empedocles' death. At the beginning of the second version we read 'Chorus of Agrigentines in the distance', but that is all. The reason, of course, is not that Hölderlin was incapable of writing choric verse—the great part of *Empedocles on Etna* is more choric than dramatic in character—but that Empedocles is not sustained by a community, as Samson is. Yet Empedocles' tragic offence, the offence with which Hermocrates rightly charges him and for which he is punished by 'separation', is precisely that he seeks this community, that 'he loves mortals too well' and has betrayed divine mysteries to the populace, as Samson has to a woman.

The close affinity of the two tragedies becomes clear as soon as we look not at the superficial aspects of Samson's offence, of Samson's strength and of Samson's vengeance or vindication, but at what they symbolize. Both works hinge on the betrayal of a mystery and a consequent loss of the power which is divine grace; and the betrayal in both cases is expiated by a form of suicide which, at the same time, represents a return to grace. To object that the form of Empedocles' death is also symbolic of his return to nature, a fusion with nature at its darkest, most elemental and most inchoate, merely brings us back to the doctrinal difference and Hölderlin's reasons for choosing this particular hero; we need not consider them at this point, any more than we need to stress Samson's much greater concern with outward reputation and honour, the social face of pride:

> . . . tell me Friends,
> Am I not sung and proverbd for a Fool
> In every street?
>
> (202–4)

This outward pride, in any case, is criticized by Manoah, who relates it to Samson's more essential and deep-rooted *hubris*, when he reproaches his son for preferring death to compromise:

> . . . perhaps
> God will relent, and quit thee all his debt;
> Who evermore approves and more accepts
> (Best pleas'd with humble and filial submission)
> Him who imploring mercy sues for life,
> Than who self-rigorous chooses death as due;
> Which argues over-just, and self-displeas'd
> For self-offence, more than for God offended.
>
> (508–15)

Empedocles' disciple Pausanias pleads with him in a similar strain, though his arguments are less cogent, because he does not understand the offence which Empedocles is determined to expiate.

Empedocles' isolation is indeed absolute, as the comparison with Samson shows. But what is more important is Samson's own repeated allusions to the nature of his offence:

> . . . who have profan'd
> The mystery of God giv'n me under pledge
> Of vow . . .
>
> (377–9)

> But I
> Gods counsel have not kept, his holy secret
> Presumptuously have publisht, impiously,
> Weakly at least, and shamefully . . .
>
> (496–9)

> . . . while I preserv'd these locks unshorn,
> The pledge of my unviolated vow.
>
> (1143–4)

Empedocles' strength, too, flows from his divine inspiration, as the Chief Priest says:

> Das hat zu mächtig ihn
> Gemacht, dass er vertraut
> Mit Göttern worden ist.

(What has made him too mighty is that he became familiar with gods.) And this is also the source of his weakness; Empedocles is the spoilt child of the gods, and, as such, becomes guilty of *hubris*, a *hubris* that takes the form of exuberance, indiscretion and excessive love:

> Der sie versteht,
> Ist stärker als die Starken,
> Und wohlbekannt ist dieser Seltne mir.
> Zu glüklich wuchs er auf;
> Ihm ist von Anbeginn
> Der eigne Sinn verwöhnt, dass ihn
> Geringes irrt; er wird as büssen,
> Dass er zu sehr geliebt die Sterblichen.

(Who understands them is stronger than the strong. And I know this rare one well. Too happily he grew up; from the beginning his will was pampered, so that little things confound him; he will regret that he loved mortal men too much). Samson was equally privileged, and equally tempted:

> I was his nursling once and choice delight,
> His destind from the womb,
> Promis'd by Heavenly message twice descending.
>
> (633–5)

> ... like a petty God
> I walkd about admir'd of all and dreaded
> On hostile ground ...
>
> (529–31)

In both tragedies there is the same 'coupling of god and man' and the same 'total separation'. Samson speaks of his 'sense of Heaven's desertion'; and it is no accident that the Chorus, however briefly and negatively, consider the notion of atheism:

> Unless there be who think not God at all,
> If any be, they walk obscure;
> For of such Doctrin never was there School
> But the heart of the Fool,
> And no man therein Doctor but himself.
>
> (295–9)

In this, as throughout the play, they faithfully respond to Samson's state of mind. Empedocles, as I have mentioned, has no chorus to support him, only his faithful but uncomprehending disciple Pausanias, who lacks all comparable assurance. Empedocles' separation, therefore, is unrelieved; and so are his doubts, which cannot be dismissed as atheism is dismissed by Samson's chorus. This greater isolation can be explained historically or biographically, in terms of Hölderlin's philosophical and religious views, his situation as a belated *sacer vates*, even of his approaching madness. Corresponding to Samson's great outcry

> O dark, dark, dark, amid the blaze of noon,
> Irrecoverably dark, total Eclipse
> Without all hope of day!
>
> (80–2)

there is Empedocles' opening lamentation:

> Weh! einsam! einsam! einsam!
> Und nimmer find' ich
> Euch, meine Götter,
> Und nimmer kehr' ich
> Zu deinen Leben, Natur!

(Oh, lonely, lonely, lonely. And nevermore I can find you, my gods, and, Nature, never return to your life.) It is easy enough to account for the parallel and the divergence by pointing out that whereas Milton was blind, Hölderlin succumbed to the impenetrable isolation of schizophrenia; but in the context of the two tragedies the darkness of Samson has exactly the same meaning as the loneliness of Empedocles. In other passages of this very monologue Empedocles also renders his separation by metaphors of light and darkness, vision and blindness:

> In meine Stille kamst du leisewandelnd,
> Fandst drinnen in der Halle Dunkel mich aus,
> Du Freundlicher! du kamst nicht unverhoft,
> Und fernher wirkend über der Erde vernahm
> Ich wohl dein Wiederkehren, schöner Tag! . . .
>
> . . . Vertrauert? bin ich ganz allein?
> Und ist es Nacht hier aussen auch am Tage?
> Der höher, denn ein sterblich Auge, sah,
> Der Blindgeschlagne tastet nun umher. . . .

(Into my stillness quietly wandering you came, deep in the darkness of the hall you sought me out, you kindly one! Nor yet unhoped for you came, but from the distance active above the earth clearly I heard you returning, glorious Day! . . . All saddened? and all alone? And is it night out here in day-time too? He who looked higher than ever did mortal eye, now blinded gropes about. . . .)

Clearly, Goethe and Schiller missed something through caring more for Milton's personality than for Samson's tragic separation —though Goethe must have been aware of both when much later he said that the play is close to the spirit of the ancients than any other modern work. The two interpretations are not mutually exclusive, though the less literal interpretation of Samson's darkness, not as Milton's, but as the loss of divine grace, is very much more to the point. One could pursue the personal parallel also and go on to speculate whether Milton, towards the end of his life, experienced doubts concerning his function as *sacer vates*, if not a crisis comparable to that which Hölderlin's tragedy undoubtedly marked. Hölderlin's *Empedocles*, amongst other things, is a self-condemnation, a condemnation also of the pride inseparable from the vocation of *sacer vates* and a *reductio ad absurdum* of pure pantheism; but here we must return for a moment to the philosophical aspects of the work.

In *Samson Agonistes* atheism is dismissed by the chorus, and mainly because there is no tradition that warrants such a creed. The philosophic idealism of Hölderlin's time was an attempt to meet the challenge of a frequently atheistic rationalism, and meet it on its own ground. The pantheism which Hölderlin shared with Schelling, and to a lesser extent with another of his co-seminarists, Hegel, was one such attempt. The second version of *The Death of Empedocles* breaks off before the end of the first act, long before the end of the 'separation', and shortly after a speech by Empedocles distinguished by a razor-edged irony as untypical of this hero as of Hölderlin; and the irony is directed at Empedocles himself. Pausanias has tried to comfort him by reminding him of his intimacy with the powers of nature and his ability to rule them as he pleases. Empedocles replies:

Recht! Alles weiss ich, alles kann ich meistern;
Wie meiner Hände Werk, erkenn' ich es
Durchaus und lenke, wie ich will,
Ein Herr der Geister, das Lebendige.
Mein ist die Welt und unterthan und dienstbar
Sind alle Kräfte mir, . . .
. . . zur Magd ist mir
Die herrnbedürftige Natur geworden,
Und hat sie Ehre noch, so ists von mir.
Was wäre denn der Himmel und das Meer
Und Inseln und Gestirn' und was vor Augen
Den Menschen alles liegt, was wär' es auch,
Diss todte Saitenspiel, gäb' ich ihm Ton

Und Sprach' und Seele nicht? was sind
Die Götter und ihr Geist, wenn ich sie nicht
Verkündige. Nun! Sage, wer bin ich?

(Quite true! I know all things, can master all; like my own handiwork I understand them thoroughly, a lord of spirits, govern as I please whatever lives. The world is mine, all powers submissive and subservient to my will, . . . Nature herself, so much in need of masters, is now my servant girl and, if she has any dignity left, owes it to me alone. And what, indeed, would Heaven be and the ocean and islands and stars and all that's set before the eyes of mortals, what would it be, this dead stringed instrument, did I nor lend it music and eloquence and soul? What are the gods, and what their spirit, if I do not proclaim them? Now tell me: who am I?)

This ironic reversion to his *hubris*, which at the same time reads like a reflection on modern science, but is rather a devastating exposure of the subjective basis of modern pantheism, and of philosophic idealism generally, may well indicate what kind of barrier it was that prevented Hölderlin from completing the tragedy. Hölderlin's subsequent development bears out the conjecture. The pure, virtually unmediated, pantheism of his Empedocles' creed—which alone made his tragic offence possible—is gradually modified in Hölderlin's prophetic poetry of the next few years; and *Empedocles on Etna* transcends tragedy because the hero has become as selfless as an oracle.

There is no reason to assume that Milton had to suffer a religious crisis of this order before he could write *Samson Agonistes*, or that only his blindness enabled him to give such noble and moving expression to the inner blindness of Samson. To do so, is to fall into the error of making Milton more 'human', more like ourselves, than he was, or of seeing him through post-Romantic spectacles, as Saurat did. What we can say is that the diction of *Samson Agonistes* combines starkness with stateliness, the colloquial phrase with the formal inversion[1] in a way that has analogies in *Paradise Regained*, but not in *Paradise Lost*, and that

[1] What I have in mind are lines like the following: 'Whom have I to complain of but myself?' (46), 'And I shall shortly be with them that rest' (598); 'Rise therefore with all speed and come along' (1316), balanced against even one-line inversions like 'Should *Israel* from *Philistian* yoke deliver' (39).

does suggest a possible change in Milton's conception of the *sacer vates*; and this is another reason why *Samson Agonistes* is less remote from Hölderlin, whose diction shows the same alternation of directness and obliqueness, conciseness and involution.

Because the later *sacer vates*, by his very nature, can hardly avoid a tragic phase, Hölderlin's failure to finish either *The Death of Empedocles* or *Empedocles on Etna* was not an absolute defeat; the tragic spirit was carried over into his last odes and elegies, the prophetic spirit into his 'hymns'. What it did mean was that tragedy as such is too essentially public an art form to be cultivated by poets whose vision could no longer be anything but esoteric. Lyrical poetry has the added advantage of brevity and compression, a consideration that is not irrelevant if we remember that the modern *sacer vates* is continually threatened by something much worse than the boos and cat-calls of his audience, or than the lack of one, namely by the 'circus animals' desertion', the reduction of all his visions to 'the foul rag-and-bone shop of the heart'. The very speed of Hölderlin's development, so hectic that in the six months' interval between the second and last *Empedocles* he passed from his tragic into his prophetic phase, points not only to his almost incredible efforts and achievements, but to the instability of the age. In its conception, Hölderlin's second *Empedocles* fragment is comparable to *Samson Agonistes*; but Milton's tragedy remains the last, and only, work of its kind.

X

CRITICISM AND THE MILTON CONTROVERSY

Bernard Bergonzi

WHAT HAS come to be called the 'Milton Controversy' is usually thought of as a strictly twentieth-century affair, associated with the names of Pound and Eliot, Leavis and Waldock, but its origins can be traced back to Milton's earliest critics. Though they were all sincere admirers of Milton, they often hedged round their admiration with a variety of reservations and qualifications. In these reservations we find the first hint of what has become the modern critical attack on Milton's established reputation. Addison, for example, wrote that Milton 'has carried our language to a greater height than any of the English poets have ever done before or after him, and made the sublimity of his style equal to that of his sentiments'. But he could also remark that 'our language sunk under him, and was unequal to that greatness of soul which furnished him with such glorious conceptions'. Johnson, whose antipathy to Milton as a man was marked, expressed his doubts about *Paradise Lost* in stronger terms: the poem 'is one of the books which the reader admires and lays down, and forgets to take up again. None ever wished it longer than it is. Its perusal is a duty rather than a pleasure'. He was unhappy about the 'perverse and pedantick principle' upon which Milton had formed his style, yet at the same time could conclude that his 'Babylonish Dialect' had been 'made by exalted genius and extensive learning the vehicle of so much instruction and so much pleasure that, like other lovers, we find grace in its deformity'.

With the Romantics the division in attitude becomes sharper. Keats observed, 'The Paradise Lost though so fine in itself is a corruption of our Language—it should be kept as it is unique—a curiosity—a beautiful and grand Curiosity. The most remarkable Production of the world.' Later in the same letter he adopts a more personal stance: 'I have but lately stood on my guard against Milton. Life to him would be death to me.' Other Romantics were prepared to admire Milton wholeheartedly, but very much on their own terms. For Blake, 'he was a true Poet and of the Devils party without knowing it'. Shelley, asserting that 'Milton's Devil as a moral being is far superior to this God', claimed that 'this bold neglect of a moral purpose is the most decisive proof of the supremacy of Milton's genius'. The Victorian Bagehot, though paying tribute to the beauties of Milton's poetry, felt that there was a radical fault in the structure of his greatest poem. '*Paradise Lost*, as a whole, is radically tainted by a vicious principle. It professes to justify the ways of God to men, to account for sin and death, and it tells you that the whole originated in a *political event* . . .' Bagehot was anticipating the detailed criticisms of the structure of *Paradise Lost* made by the late A. J. A. Waldock, just as Johnson's and Keat's reservations about the poem's diction were to be amplified by Eliot and Leavis.

There is no need to multiply such familiar quotations, particularly as I am concerned with the Milton Controversy as it has arisen in the last thirty years. Yet two points need to be noted: though earlier critics may sometimes have felt, with Eliot, that 'while it must be admitted that Milton is a very great poet indeed, it is something of a puzzle to decide in what his greatness consists', they had no essential doubts about the greatness itself. They were content to let Milton remain in the front rank of English poets, alongside Shakespeare; they were certain of his pre-eminence, whatever reservations they had about particular aspects of his work. In this they were supported by the undisputed fact of Milton's survival as a national classic, a survival which had more to do with the untutored instincts of innumerable 'ordinary' readers than with the precise formulation of critical difficulties. And Milton still survives: the mere existence of a Milton Controversy at all proves this. Yet, to come to my second point, though the origins of the modern critical attack on Milton can be found in the more or less random observations of earlier writers, this attack is much more systematic, and its exponents have had the aim—implicit or explicit—of reducing Milton's stature as an English classic. F. R. Leavis wrote in *Revaluation* in 1936 of 'Milton's dislodgement . . . after two centuries of predominance . . .' 'Dislodgement' was conceived of as a desirable aim, even though there might be some doubt as to whether it had actually been achieved. Milton was still allowed considerable merit, it was true, and the word 'genius' was freely applied to him, but he was to be firmly removed to a lesser eminence on the English Parnassus.

Many critics have adopted an anti-Miltonic position in the first half of the present century: Middleton Murry, Herbert Read and Ezra Pound have all expressed grave doubts or positive objections to Milton's pre-eminence as a poet. But the full weight of the attack on Milton's established reputation can, I think, be located in three specific documents: T. S. Eliot's 'A Note on the Verse of John Milton', first published in *Essays and Studies* in 1936; F. R. Leavis's essay in *Revaluation*, 'Milton's Verse' (to which must be added his subsequent essays, 'Mr. Eliot and Milton' and 'In Defence of Milton', included in *The Common Pursuit*, 1952); and A. J. A. Waldock's book, *Paradise Lost and its Critics*, published in 1947. I shall confine my attention to these three works, and in particular to those by Leavis and Waldock. Mr. Eliot, in fact, attempted a refutation of his own criticisms in his British Academy lecture on Milton delivered in 1947, though one must remark in passing that it is rather less impressive as a critical performance than his first essay. The essence of Eliot's changed position was that in 1936 he thought that Milton could only be a thoroughly bad example for poets, whereas in 1947 he had come to think that he might be rather a good one. We are increasingly seeing Eliot's critical writings—the best of them, at least—as the working observations of a practising poet, rather than as the *ex cathedra* pronouncements of an infallible leader of literary taste, and the change seems to me all to the good. Eliot, in his criticism, accepted what he could use—Donne, Dante, Baudelaire—and rejected what he could not: Milton, above all. Much the same is true of Pound in his constant anti-Miltonic sniping. Both of these poets were doing no more than demonstrate that Milton was quite useless to them in the kind of poetry they wished to write. Which is an eminently reasonable attitude. Keats had done the same thing when he remarked that 'Life to him would be death to me'.

But Leavis and Waldock, as academic critics and teachers, were inevitably involved in a more public relation to literature than poets like Pound or Eliot. One must insist on this, despite Leavis's commitment to Eliot's own pragmatic concept of 'Tradition'. It was mainly in academic circles that their formulations were propounded, and accepted or rejected. And here we are at the core of the modern controversy. In an essay published in *Scrutiny* in 1952, 'Reflections on the Milton Controversy', Mr. John Peter surveyed the debate as it had developed up to that time. He complained that whereas many academics had continued to treat Milton as a pre-eminently great poet, as though his reputation had never been in question, and without attempting to justify it critically, the cogent demonstrations made by Leavis and Waldock of positive weaknesses in the verse and structure of *Paradise Lost* had been simply ignored. 'We might say that it is no disparagement of the work of critics like F. R. Leavis and A. J. A. Waldock to claim that, if today their verdict on *Paradise Lost* as a poem at best only partially successful seems irrefutable, that is partly because those who admire the poem have done so little to meet this verdict in anything like a cogent way.' Peter, in short, claimed that there had been something like a conspiracy of silence among academics and professional admirers of Milton, a deliberate refusal to recognize, let alone to answer, the—to him—irrefutable adverse criticisms of Leavis and Waldock. More recently a similar charge was made by Leavis himself in a letter to the *Times Literary Supplement*, 19th September, 1958. There he claimed that the situation had not changed since Peter's article appeared: the 'Miltonists' consistently ignored his and Waldock's criticisms, or pretended, wrongly, that they had already been disposed of. The anti-Miltonists, it seems, would assert that there has never been a Milton controversy in the strict sense. Specific and detailed criticisms of Milton have been offered, but the upholders of Milton's established reputation have refused to enter in debate. If this is true, a heavy charge is laid upon the 'Miltonists'. At the very least they can be accused of a lack of intellectual integrity, if not of positive moral shabbiness. I want now to examine this question and to see if there is any reason why the anti-Miltonic arguments should have gone unanswered for so many years. For reasons of clarity I should make it plain that my own bias is pro- rather than anti-Milton. That is to say, though, like many earlier critics, I have reservations about certain particulars, I have never had any difficulty in accepting the traditional view of Milton as one of the greatest poets in the language, and *Paradise Lost* as a supreme masterpiece. I might add, as a purely empirical note, that this conviction has been strengthened by having recently spent a year in teaching Milton to undergraduates, which entailed a good deal of close examination and detailed discussion of his poetry. Nevertheless, the adverse criticisms of Milton made by Leavis and Waldock seem to me sufficiently serious to deserve careful consideration, and, if possible a reasoned answer.

For Leavis, in the first instance, the 'dislodgement' of Milton had been effected by the creative achievement of Eliot's poetry, which 'gave his few critical asides—potent, it is true, by context—their finality, and made it unnecessary to elaborate a case'. Here we have an interesting example of Leavis's rather extreme underwriting of Eliot's concept of 'Tradition' as a living and ever-changing thing, in which the successful creative work can modify our whole approach to the literature of the past. It was a plausible and attractive notion, and one which was essential for Eliot's own poetic achievement, but in the last forty years it has hardened into a critical dogma of extreme rigidity, and it seems to me that it might profitably be re-examined, though this is not the place to do it. However, by 1936 Leavis felt that excessive claims were once more being made for Milton and that it was, after all, necessary to elaborate a case against him. Anyone trying to reproduce Leavis's arguments has to face the difficulty that he is very attached to the integrity of his own verbal formulations and is apt to denounce any summary of his views as mere distortion or wilful misrepresentation, usually for the worst of motives. However, I shall do my best to reproduce the gist of Leavis's case against Milton as presented in *Revaluation*, in his own words as far as possible. It is, essentially, an objection to the whole Miltonic habit of language: 'our objection to Milton, it must be insisted, is that we dislike his verse . . .' Leavis goes on to give detailed examples of precisely what he dislikes. The whole movement of Milton's verse is not expressive but mechanical and ritualistic: 'the pattern, the stylized gesture and movement, has no particular expressive work to do, but functions by rote, of its own momentum, in the manner of a ritual.' Milton's 'Grand Style' is, in fact, a 'tyrannical stylization'. A few passages are held up to admiration but not very many: 'Even in the first two books of *Paradise Lost*, where the myth has vigorous life and one can admire the magnificent invention that Milton's verse is, we feel, after a few hundred lines, our sense of dissatisfaction growing into something stronger.' In the Mulciber passage at the end of Book i the characteristic ritualistic movement of the verse does permit—more or less by accident, it seems—a genuinely expressive and felicitous effect, 'where the verse glows with an unusual life'. And something similar is true of the lines on 'Proserpin gath'ring flowers' from Book iv. High praise is indeed given to the temptation speech from *Comus*, but for being in essentials un-Miltonic: 'It shows, in fact, the momentary presence in Milton of Shakespeare.' Leavis's whole objection to the Miltonic Grand Style is that it does not permit any subtle and sensitive expression of the movements of actual sensory experience. In general, the verse does not 'act out' what it describes, and we are fixated at a purely verbal level: 'He exhibits a feeling *for* words rather than a capacity for feeling *through* words; we are often, in reading him, moved to comment that he is "external" or that he "works from the outside".'

By way of an illustrative example Leavis compares a plangent passage from 'Lycidas'—where the words 'seem, comparatively, to be occupied with valuing themselves rather than with doing anything'—with some tough and knotty lines from Donne's 'Third Satyre' ('On a huge hill / Cragged, and steep, Truth stands . . .'), where the words imitate precisely what they describe. 'This,' says Leavis, of the Donne passage, 'is the Shakespearean use of English; one might say that it is the English use—the use, in the essential spirit of the language, of its characteristic resources.' By being so removed from ordinary idiomatic language, Milton was incapable of achieving the kind of necessary subtlety of movement that comes from playing the movements of the speaking voice against the structure of the verse.

> The extreme and consistent remoteness of Milton's medium from any English that was ever spoken is an immediately relevant consideration. It became, of course, habitual to him;

but habituation could not sensitize a medium so cut off from speech—speech that belongs to the emotional and sensory texture of actual living and is in resonance with the nervous system; it could only confirm an impoverishment of sensibility. In any case, the Grand Style barred Milton from essential expressive resources of English that he had once commanded.

In conclusion, Leavis claims that Milton's strength is of the kind normally associated with character rather than intelligence, and that this defect of intelligence was also a defect of imagination.

I shall defer discussion of Leavis's case for a little, though it is worth noting that it is not a mere critical reappraisal of Milton, but a whole-scale demolition. It is hard to see what would be left of Milton as a serious writer if one assented to it in its entirety, apart from a few occasional passages that 'glow with an unusual life'. Tributes paid to the 'magnificent invention' of Milton's verse, or the 'consummate art' of 'Lycidas', are rather perfunctory if the invention and the art are used in such a thoroughly mistaken fashion. After all, if 'a poem is made out of words' and a poet's use of words is demonstrably and disastrously wrong, what is left of the poem? John Peter, in the essay from which I have already quoted, is somewhat disingenuous when he remarks, 'Neither Dr. Leavis nor the late Professor Waldock has, after all, branded Milton as worthless'. True, but they have not left him worth very much, either.

Leavis's attack on Milton's language is paralleled by A. J. A. Waldock's criticisms of the underlying structure of *Paradise Lost*. Rather than attempt to summarize the whole of his closely-argued book, I shall reproduce a lengthy passage from his first chapter in which he sets out, clearly and fully, his approach.

It is possible, I think, to overrate very much Milton's *awareness* of the peculiar difficulties of his theme. The difficulties are of the kind that fairly leap to our eyes. That is partly because, owing to certain types of literary development during the last two centuries or so, we have received an intensive training in the business of estimating the sort of literary problem that is radical in *Paradise Lost*. We have acquired, in plain fact—through the novel, and in other ways—certain types of literary experience that Milton was without. It is not absurd to mention the novel in connection with *Paradise Lost*, for the problems of such a poem and the characteristic problems of the novel have much in common. The novel has given us an enormous store of precedents. Largely as a result of its history we have built up a technique for assessing at once the practicability of certain themes for literary treatment, a technique that it is not ridiculous to suggest that Milton did not possess in quite the same sense. We have only to look at the material that he was bent on disposing in his epic to see that some of the problems he faced were virtually insoluble. A glance at the story of the Fall as it is given in Genesis shows that it is lined with difficulties of the gravest order. God, to begin with, does not show to advantage in that particular story: the story is a bad one for God. Within that set of events to make God attractive to our common human sensibilities (and it is not to be forgotten that the *raison d'etre* of the whole poem lies in its appeal to common human sensibilities) will be hard. Again, it will be necessary to mark the transition from innocence to guilt; somehow sinlessness has to give place to sin; and in a large narrative such a transition may not be easy to make plausible. There is, once more, the disproportion (cruel at least on the face of it) between the offence and the punishment—bringing us back again to God. That apparent disproportion may not trouble us in the biblical story, the miniature; but what of it when the story is magnified a hundred times? Looking back at *Paradise Lost* from what in some real senses is our vantage-point and bringing to bear on it, quite frankly, the whole weight of our own literary experience, we almost catch our breath at the manifold drawbacks of the fable. Could any writer with an instinct for narrative, we ask ourselves, have failed to see what problems those first three chapters of Genesis held, and to shrink back deterred? At half-a-dozen points difficulties lie in wait that at the slightest prompting might become acute. The story in Genesis was like a stretch of film minutely flawed. Milton's plan was to take this and project it on an enormous canvas. Must he not (we wonder sometimes) have foreseen the effect of the tremendous enlargement: that every slight imperfection would show, that every rift would become a gulf?[1]

[1] A. J. A. Waldock, *Paradise Lost and Its Critics* (1947), pp. 17–19.

Milton, Waldock concludes, foresaw nothing of the kind; but the modern reader has the advantage of him.

In the ensuing chapters Waldock works out the implications of his approach by detailed analysis: God is seen to come off very badly indeed in the poem; the business of the temptation and fall does indeed violate our 'common human sensibilities', particularly when we are asked to condemn Adam for following Eve in eating the forbidden fruit when his motive for doing so was simply human love of the highest kind; the punishment they receive is cruel and disproportionate; and Satan, having become much too impressive and interesting in the first two books is systematically degraded in the rest of the poem. Many of these ideas can be found in earlier critics of Milton, notably Shelley and Bagehot, but Waldock applies them far more assiduously and systematically. In the course of doing so, he finds something profoundly wrong at the very heart of the poem's narrative structure: '*Paradise Lost* cannot take the strain at its centre, it breaks there, the theme is too much for it.'[1] In his final chapter he rather unconvincingly tries to salvage something for lovers of Milton to content themselves with: 'We shall go on reading the poem for ever, I presume, for the glory of the writing and for the spirit of Milton that so lives in whatever he wrote.' But the 'glory of the writing' would scarcely satisfy many future readers if Leavis's account of it was a true one. A couple of pages later Waldock adds that *Paradise Lost* 'has enough left, in all conscience, to stay it against anything that we can do'. Leavis who refers to *Paradise Lost and Its Critics* as 'by far the best book on Milton I have read', objects to this perfunctory gesture: 'But what is there left? There are the first two books, which are of a piece and grandly impressive, and, in the others, numbers of "beauties" major or minor.'[2] Elsewhere Leavis complains that Waldock doesn't draw the consequence of his findings but adds in a footnote that the late Professor Waldock had told him in a letter 'that of course he hadn't drawn the consequence of his findings: he daren't; he was afraid enough about what he *had* done'.

Here, then, we have in essentials the modern two-pronged critical attack on the pre-eminence of *Paradise Lost*: Leavis on the

[1] Waldock, p. 56.

[2] *The Common Pursuit* (1952), p. 27.

language of its verse, and Waldock on its theme and structure. It is indeed a radical one: if the language and structure of the poem are both so unsatisfactory then hardly anything worth considering of literary interest remains of what had previously been considered the greatest non-dramatic long poem in the language. One might as well hand it over in its entirety to the philologists and the historians of ideas. And, as the anti-Miltonists insist, no attempt has been made to defend the poem in the same detailed and specific manner in which it has been attached.

A partial exception must be here made for C. S. Lewis's book, *A Preface to Paradise Lost*, which first appeared in 1942. This is an interesting and valuable little book. It was partly written, one assumes, to counter Leavis's attack on Milton, but it is in no sense a work of detailed criticism, and Peter and Waldock have no difficulty in disposing of it rather rapidly. Professor Lewis's book was intended primarily to supply the historical dimension which most modern readers of Milton lack, and it is a mine of information on such subjects as epic diction, Augustinian theology, and Renaissance ideas about angels, to name but a few. Yet Lewis was not able to resist the temptation to play the public moralist from time to time, using the text of *Paradise Lost* as a basis for disquisitions on God and Man and human society in general. And his characteristic manner of blandly jollying along his reader, though engaging in short stretches, becomes rather tiresome in the long run. One of Lewis's central assumptions (and it is here that he seems to be directing himself towards Leavis's criticisms) is that if we really understand the principles governing the epic diction in which *Paradise Lost* is written, and if we know something of the ideas expressed in it, then we cannot help but find it a great poem. It is certainly useful, or even essential, to know these things, but no amount of sheer knowledge can precipitate into a positive judgement in quite such a simple fashion. And some of his assumptions are questionable, or at least excessively simplified. Thus, Lewis writes of epic diction, 'Once the diction has been established it works of itself. Almost anything the poet wants to say, has only to be turned into this orthodox and ready-made diction and it becomes poetry. "Whatever Miss T. eats turns into Miss T."' What kind of poetry, one is entitled to ask. Lewis is here using the word 'poetry' in a descriptive and not an evaluative sense, but presumably some kinds of epic diction are better than others, even when judged by the most rigid historical canons. There seems to be no reason why Lewis's diction-machine should not produce bad poetry as well as good, and the whole matter is far too generalized to be of much help to the would-be reader of *Paradise Lost*.

In a later chapter Lewis refers to Leavis's criticisms, and makes a very significant comment, to which I shall return:

> Dr. Leavis does not differ from me about the properties of Milton's epic verse. He describes them very accurately . . . It is not that he and I see different things when we look at *Paradise Lost*. He sees and hates the very same that I see and love. Hence the disagreement between us tends to escape from the realm of literary criticism. We differ not about the nature of Milton's poetry, but about the nature of man, or even the nature of joy itself.

It would be tempting to spend longer on *A Preface to Paradise Lost*, which is a provocative work in a number of ways, but I merely wish to establish that it has not been accepted by the anti-Miltonists as providing the positive and detailed answer to their criticisms that they have demanded. It does not, in short, meet them on their own ground.

I will now suggest that the reason why these criticisms have remained unanswered in any detailed way for so long is not necessarily because of sloth or bad faith on the opposing side, but because they are, quite simply, *unanswerable*. That is to say, they are unanswerable within the terms of reference in which they are made. In order to see why this is so it will be necessary to see what is meant by the concept of 'answering' a critical judgement. The critical judgement, we are often told, is not a question of externally applying standards to a work, but is the product of a personal or existential encounter between the critic and the work, in which he tries to reproduce as faithfully and honestly as possible his response to it and whatever conviction of value may be part of that response. It will involve the whole personality of the critic: his intelligence and sensibility and the accumulated experience he can bring to bear. So much may be accepted as axiomatic. He will, of course, have his particular convictions and presuppositions about life and literature, but he should not be particularly aware of them when he is making his response; they will, rather, be present as informing his mind and personality when he makes his judgement. This is true, but at the same time one must insist that these convictions and presuppositions will have a great deal to do with determining both the form of the response and the way in which his judgement is formulated. Any critic, no matter how open-minded he thinks himself to be, will inevitably go to a work looking for certain things, and his judgement will be conditioned by the extent to which he does or does not find them. What these determining factors are will be apparent from the critic's major descriptive or evaluative terms. These terms, and the critic's mode of articulating them, will form a distinctive 'critical language', no matter how personal and apparently untheoretical his approach to literary works may be. The critic who, in the manner of Bradley, discusses a Shakespeare play primarily in terms of character will clearly be using a different 'critical language' from the critic who sees it primarily in terms of themes and images. Again, those critics of a past generation who seemed to be mainly interested in the 'verbal music' of lyric poetry were obviously not using the same language as those more modern ones who prefer to concentrate their attention on such qualities as 'irony' or 'ambiguity'. The critic's response, in short, will necessarily be determined by the kind of 'critical language' he habitually uses, even though he may be quite unconscious of its implications. As R. S. Crane has written:

> It is not a sufficient objection to this view of criticism that it has rarely been entertained even by the most self-conscious of critics. For the diversities of language we are here concerned with are matters of assumed principle, definition, and method, such as are not likely to show themselves, save indirectly, on the surface of a critic's discourse, and hence not likely, even in controversy, to force themselves on his attention. They pertain rather to what he thinks *with* than to what he thinks *about*—to the implicit structure and rationale of his argument as a whole than to the explicit doctrines he is attempting to state.[1]

[1] R. S. Crane, *The Languages of Criticism and the Structure of Poetry* (1953), p. 13. Professor Crane's account of the multiplicity of critical languages seems to me very illuminating, even though he is prepared to accept a degree of pluralism and relativism that is theoretically plausible but would present grave difficulties in practice.

We may conclude, then, that a fruitful debate can only take place between critics who are using the same critical language (just as any genuine intellectual argument must imply a certain agreement about basic premises). A critic of a rather simple-minded sort who complained of a total absence of Tennysonian verbal music in Donne's poetry (and who presumably had made good his complaint by analysis and quotation) could only be answered to his satisfaction by another critic who was prepared to argue, in some spirit of misguided ingenuity, that such verbal music *could* after all be detected in Donne. This is a deliberately simple and even absurd example, but its very simplicity should make the point clear. Insistence on the terms of reference of a particular critical language can easily pre-judge the issue.

We may now return to the Milton Controversy. When the anti-Miltonists demand an 'answer' to their charges, they are undoubtedly expecting an answer couched in the language in which these charges were made: otherwise they would not be able to recognize it as an answer at all. Leavis or Peter might be satisfied by an opponent who tries to show that Milton's Grand Style *did* possess the qualities of sensitivity and subtlety and expressive closeness to the movements of actual sensory experience that Leavis has so convincingly denied to it; but not otherwise. And it is most unlikely that anyone would be found to make the attempt. Leavis has certainly established that these qualities are *not* present in Milton's verse in the way that they are in much of Shakespeare's, and even such a convinced Miltonist as Professor Lewis has paid tribute to the accuracy of Leavis's account of Milton's verse. Within the limits of his particular critical language Leavis's attack is irrefutable. Similarly with Waldock's criticisms. A successful answer to Waldock would have to show that narrative structure of *Paradise Lost does* possess the kind of coherence and psychological plausibility that we have come to expect from the novel. Again, there can be no doubt that it does not.

But the anti-Miltonic arguments, though unanswerable, are also wrong. Wrong because, to speak for myself, they do not correspond with the facts of my literary experience; nor, I imagine with those of many other readers: certainly undergraduates with whom I have discussed Milton's poetry seem to find more to admire than to dislike in it, and to remain unconvinced by the arguments of Leavis and Waldock (which I have recommended them to read). The literary judgement that is generally regarded as both unanswerable and wrong is by no means uncommon in literary history. A classical example would be Thomas Rymer's vigorously argued and well-illustrated demolition of *Othello*, of which Mr. Eliot has remarked in a characteristic aside, 'I have never, by the way, seen a cogent refutation'.[1] A more modern instance is Henry James's description of the novels of Tolstoy and Dostoevsky as 'great fluid puddings'. Though made merely as a casual remark in a letter, it fits very readily into the context of James's more systematic writings about fiction: it is, in fact, a perfectly coherent observation in the 'critical language' of one who was both a great novelist and a major critic of his art. Nevertheless, most readers would probably find it wrong or at least totally irrelevant to the kind of experience they get from reading Tolstoy or Dostoevsky.

The only useful fashion in which the anti-Milton case can be answered, I think, is on a second-order level: that is to say, by examining the appropriateness or otherwise of the formulations in which it is expressed. This is not easy and it may strike some as unfair: an exchange of the relatively straightforward business of criticism for the devious processes of metacriticism. But one should surely follow an argument wherever it leads, if there is a possible hope of clearing up an area of confusion.

If we read carefully through Leavis's essay on Milton, we soon become aware that his major evaluative terms are 'expressive', 'subtle' or 'subtlety', 'sensitive' or 'sensitiveness'. These, it appears, are the qualities which Leavis values above all in poetic language and which Milton conspicuously lacks. Whether his use of the word 'expressive' points to an unlikely (one would have thought) link with the aesthetics of Croce I do not know; but in general one can assert that these three terms are all closely linked with the 'organicist' or 'vitalist' kind of metaphorical thinking that underlies much of Leavis's critical writing (and which is expressed elsewhere in his celebrated use of the word 'life' as a major evaluative term of absolute and unquestionable value). For Leavis, the language of poetry should follow as closely and expressively as possible the subtle and delicate movements of actual sensory experience. Ideally we should not be aware of the words

[1] *Selected Essays* (1932), p. 141.

as words at all; rather, we should be 'directly aware of a tissue of feelings and perceptions'. Effective poetic language should be fairly close to speech, to 'speech that belongs to the emotional and sensory texture of actual living and is in resonance with the nervous system'. The last phrase seems to indicate a clear cross-reference to the ideas of Richards as expressed in *Principles of Literary Criticism*. This closeness to what he calls 'the emotional and sensory texture of actual living' is, it will be apparent, an informing principle—if not *the* informing principle—in Leavis's criticism. Literature should present us with an enlargement and refinement of the recognizable elements in our own experience, where the language itself enacts these elements. Hence his marked preference for an 'expressive' as against a 'ritualistic' use of language. This is a perfectly intelligible view of literature, but it leaves out far too much. It quite fails to account for the perennial human desire for the kind of art that asserts itself as *art*, as something avowedly *other* than the elements of normal human experience, and which opposes and limits them. Such art, normally expressed in a hieratic form or as ritual, offers an escape from the prison which the flux of common human experience may, at times, legitimately be taken as being. Speaking in a general way one might perhaps call this kind of art 'religious', but I am now only concerned with it as a psychological reality. The rhythms of Milton's verse, as Leavis shows by a good deal of scrupulous analysis, are non-organic, and its mode of procedure—particularly in *Paradise Lost*—is ritualistic. It is Leavis's *a priori* distaste for such modes that leads him to make his resolutely unfavourable judgement on Milton.

Why Leavis should hold the view of literary art that he does is, of course, a question far removed from the confines of criticism as Professor Lewis has already recognized. I see no reason why the conditioning elements of the Leavisian *Weltanschauung* should not be discussed as a subject of great interest in itself, though this is hardly the occasion for it. Nothing would give me greater pleasure than the spectacle of Professor Lewis and Dr. Leavis publicly debating 'the nature of man, or even the nature of joy itself', unlikely though it is to happen. Yet if Leavis's case against *Paradise Lost* is to be answered by those who find it wrong or inadequate, it must, I think, be approached in some such general and admittedly 'extra-literary' fashion, before attempting a reading of the poem based in a larger and more inclusive conception of literature.

The assumptions which condition Waldock's criticisms of *Paradise Lost* are, initially at least, of a more specifically literary kind: they are stated in the passage which I have already quoted. There he writes: 'We have acquired, in plain fact—through the novel, and in other ways—certain types of literary experience that Milton was without. It is not absurd to mention the novel in connection with *Paradise Lost*, for the problems of such a poem and the characteristic problems of the novel have elements in common.' If one found this statement in an undergraduate essay one might scribble a question mark in the margin and ask for some evidence. The assumption is absolutely central to Waldock's approach to the poem: it seems to me far from self-evident, but he gives no reasons for making it. Waldock uses it to deduce a monistic conception of 'narrative' which can apply equally to the epic poem and the realistic novel, and which is, in fact, so attenuated as to be entirely useless. Waldock's approach is somewhat reminiscent of William Archer's decision that the New Drama of Ibsen gave one good grounds to make a reappraisal of Shakespeare and his contemporaries in the light of the more advanced modern knowledge of dramatic techniques: they, of course, came off rather badly. The fact is that the modern novel deals, for the most part, with men, and in their fallen state, rather than supernatural or prelapsarian beings. Behaviour in the novel is inevitably involved with a complex of assumptions relating to an existing order of society, and the conventions governing the form are all intensely naturalistic. Any concept of 'narrative' that can be drawn from the novel must inevitably be affected by these conditions, and nothing could be more certain than that it would be wholly inapplicable to such a poem as *Paradise Lost*. Waldock assiduously analyses the structure of *Paradise Lost* as though it *were* a novel, and the result, though often interesting, is singularly unconvincing.

Waldock's determination to read *Paradise Lost* like a novel has one significant aspect: his commitment to the kind of moral naturalism that is the dominant ethic of modern fiction (this phrase may not be altogether clear: I mean simply that the novel does not easily contain supernatural elements, and is generally resistant to specifically religious ideas). He reads *Paradise*

Lost, in short, not merely as if Christianity were not true, but as though it had never existed. I do not think that Christian *belief* is necessary for an appreciation of *Paradise Lost*; the reverse, if anything (as a Christian myself I find Milton's religious ideas and attitudes so uncongenial that I have to try to put them out of mind when reading him) but the reader should, after all, have some access to the Christian *sensibility* that has been an informing element in over a thousand years of Western literature. Waldock, however, approaches the poem with no more than the typical assumptions of most modern novel readers: i.e. that we are going to read a naturalistic story about people rather like ourselves in a recognizable setting. He is fairly specific about this: 'all that is necessary in reading the poem is to attend carefully to our impressions, because it is these that constitute the facts of the poem.' He continues, in a passage that suggests a rather surprising degree of critical slackness, 'Between the impressions of natural, easygoing, unprejudiced readers there is, I believe, no great variation. Differences mount with sophistication—because the registering mind, so to say, comes to know too much'.[1] In other words, one needs to read *Paradise Lost* with as little knowledge as possible of its substance. Many scholars, I think, assume that we need to know too much before we can appreciate *Paradise Lost*, but Waldock certainly errs in the opposite direction. Waldock's 'natural, easygoing, unprejudiced' reader would, in certain important respects, not be unprejudiced at all; he would inevitably be prejudiced *against* the poem in respect of the sensibility that informs it, and the result would be incomprehension. Waldock's book exhibits precisely this incomprehension at some length.

There is a good example of his failure of sensibility in his discussion of Adam's crucial speech in Book ix, immediately after the Fall. It concludes:

> However I with thee have fixt my Lot,
> Certain to undergo like doom; if Death
> Consort with thee, Death is to mee as Life;
> So forcible within my heart I feel
> The Bond of Nature draw me to my own,
> My own in thee, for what thou art is mine;

[1] Waldock, p. 26.

> Our State cannot be severd, we are one,
> One Flesh; to lose thee were to lose my self.
>
> (952–59)

Waldock comments on the intensity of feeling conveyed in the speech, and says that its dominant emotion is not—as other critics have suggested—merely 'comradeship' or 'gregariousness' or 'uxoriousness': it is, he insists (rightly I think), *love* of the highest human kind. He then quotes Milton's subsequent description of Adam as 'fondly overcome with Femal charm', and claims that the contempt expressed in this line clashes violently with the tender feelings informing Adam's speech. Milton, he suggests, is *imposing* on us the view we ought to take but without any emotional conviction. Here Waldock, by insisting on his reading of *Paradise Lost* as a simple naturalistic narrative, is being grossly imperceptive. In these lines we are faced with one of those profound paradoxes that lie at the heart, not only of *Paradise Lost*, but of the whole Western and Christian tradition. Man ought always to prefer the highest love there is—Divine love—to the highest love he knows—human love. But very frequently he does not, and who can blame him for it? Adam, in this situation was *both* acting upon the highest possible human motives, and 'fondly overcome with Femal charm'. On the human level—which is Milton's level, for *Paradise Lost* is not an essentially religious poem at all—there is no solution to this paradox. We are meant to feel the sense of strain and contradiction that Waldock complains of, for the situation that Milton presents is a sadly common part of the experience of fallen man. It has been expressed by many Christian moralists:

> Oh wearisome Condition of Humanity!
> Borne under one Law to another bound:
> Vainly begot, and yet forbidden vanity,
> Created sicke, commanded to be sound.

One does not need to be a believing Christian to feel the force of this, I think; it is merely sufficient to have some sense of what it feels like to have a Christian conscience. But this seems to be beyond Waldock: for him the whole sensibility informing *Paradise Lost* belongs to some obscure private mythology invented by

Milton, which we must resolutely ignore in case it interferes with our 'impressions' of the narrative, which 'constitute the facts of the poem'. Waldock's assumption that *Paradise Lost* is to be read like a novel causes him not only to misconstrue its narrative structure, but also to approach the poem with the kind of moral naturalism that is quite appropriate when dealing with works of fiction but is wholly inappropriate when discussing *Paradise Lost* —or, indeed, most other major works of literature published before about 1700.

I have tried to examine the modern Milton Controversy and to show that the anti-Miltonic arguments are, in terms of the 'critical languages' in which they are expressed, unanswerable. Following from this, I have claimed that these arguments are, nevertheless, unsatisfactory by showing the insufficiency of the criteria determining them. I am not likely to have convinced those who, like John Peter, find Waldock's and Leavis's case 'irrefutable', but I hope I may have shown those who are still undecided a new way of looking at the matter.

To negate a negation is not to make out a positive case for anything. *Paradise Lost* is in urgent need of the kind of attention that will make it once more critically available to the modern reader; but it is not my place to attempt it here. I have had strictly limited aims in this essay, which is already too long. Leavis has remarked that 'Milton has been made the keep of an anti-critical defensive system', and I may expect the charge that in demonstrating the limitations of certain modes of Milton criticism I am opposed to criticism itself. I can only say in advance that this is not so, and that I have no interest at all in upholding the sort of flaccid academicism that has been prevalent for so long in Milton studies. I think a sound critical case can and should be made out for Milton's traditional reputation, which would at the same time take note of his limitations, even though these would appear as far less fundamentally damaging than Leavis or Waldock have claimed. Such a case might, for instance, propose that the theme of *Paradise Lost* is indeed 'loss of Eden', and that the imaginative centre of the poem is to be found in Books iv and ix: its meaning might well have a good deal to do with what Freudians call the 'birth trauma', the expulsion from the womb into a world where life and death are inextricably mixed.